W9-CBA-506

Serving
with the Poor in
Latin America

Tetsunao Yamamori, Bryant L. Myers, C. René Padilla and Greg Rake, editors

MARC

A division of World Vision International
800 West Chestnut Avenue, Monrovia, California 91016-3198 USA

Other books in this series:
Serving with the Poor in Asia
Serving with the Poor in Africa

Serving with the Poor in Latin America
Tetsunao Yamamori, Bryant L. Myers, C. René Padilla and Greg Rake, editors

ISBN 1-887983-03-1

Published by MARC, a division of World Vision International, 800 West Chestnut Avenue, Monrovia, California 91016, U.S.A.

Printed in the United States of America. Editor and typesetter: Edna G. Valdez. Cover design: Richard Sears. Cover photo: Terri Owens, World Vision.

Contents

Part Three - Conclusion

Appendixes

Editors and contributors

Tetsunao Yamamori, Ph.D., is president of Food for the Hungry International (FHI). He has taught in the fields of sociology, international development and missiology. Currently he serves as adjunct professor of sociology at Arizona State University and visiting professor of missiology at Tokyo Christian University.

Bryant L. Myers, Ph.D., is vice president for Strategy and Christian Mission at World Vision International, and executive director of MARC (Mission Advanced Research and Communication Center). He is the author of *The New Context of World Mission* and *The Changing Shape of World Mission*.

C. René Padilla, Ph.D., was born in Ecuador and has lived in Argentina since 1967. He has served as general secretary for the Latin American Theological Fraternity. He is president of the Kairos Foundation in Buenos Aires and pastor of a Baptist church.

Greg Rake, M.A., coordinated the Latin America Consultation for Holistic Ministry. He is director of the Americas for the Mennonite Board of Missions and Commission of Overseas Missions. He has served in Latin America since 1974 with the Mennonite Central Committee in Bolivia and with Project Concern.

Enrique Martínez is from Honduras, where he is the medical director for the Evangelical Hospital in Siguatepeque. He received his medical degree in Honduras, is a member of the pastoral team of the Betel Church and coordinator of the Theological Fraternity in Siguatepeque.

Alexis Andino was born in Tegucigalpa, Honduras. He is trained as an agricultural science specialist, has worked for eleven years in community development with Christian agencies in Honduras and is director of CONSEDE.

Claudio Oliver was born in Rio de Janeiro, Brazil. He was trained as a dentist. He is pastor of the Community of Christ Church in Curitiba, involved in a project that is "part of our life and vocation."

Denise da Silva Maranháo was born into a Christian family in São Paulo, Brazil. She was a member of the University Student Movement, where she felt called to mission. She is a social worker for the past twelve years in the project "New Life for the Children," in the rural town of Sabinopolis.

Uriel Tercero was born in Nicaragua. He is trained as a pastor and was forced to leave his first pastorate due to war-related circumstances. He works as a pastor and an agronomist, and supervises churches of the Assemblies of God in his region.

Rosa Camargo is a Colombian. She and her husband serve under the Latin American Mission of Canada in Barranquilla, Colombia. She is a social worker, and has studied in Israel to observe cooperatives and income-generating projects.

Débora de Arco was born in Colombia. She has worked in development projects for many years, and was most recently appointed as director of education and development for World Vision in Colombia. She holds a degree in social work and adult education.

Ivan Delgado is a civil engineer and a computer technician. He was born in Oruro, Bolivia. He is a deacon in the Assembly of God church and works as regional supervisor for FHI in Bolivia.

Atilio Quintanilla is a member of the Christian and Missionary Alliance church in Lima, Peru. He has a passion for working with families and, with his wife Ana, has developed a ministry of "orientation and counseling for families." He has been with FHI in Peru for the past five years.

Alva Couto was born to a Christian family in Minas Gerais, Brazil. She is a social worker who serves as associate director of the Instituto Polus in Belo Horizonte, Brazil. She is a member of the Presbyterian Church and of the Latin American Theological Fraternity, Brazil Chapter.

Javier Mayorga was born in Guatemala and lives in Costa Rica. He has a degree in civil and sanitation engineering and an MBA from the University of Francisco Marroquín. He has worked with World Vision in a variety of positions.

Introduction

Tetsunao Yamamori

Welcome to the third in our series of books on holistic ministry. This book follows *Serving with the Poor in Asia* (MARC 1995) and *Serving with the Poor in Africa* (MARC 1996). The final one in the current series will be on holistic ministry among the urban poor. The book will be called "Serving with the Poor in the City." Acquaintance with all these books will benefit the reader in acquiring a comprehensive view of what God is doing at the frontier of world mission today.

The Latin America Consultation

Quito, Ecuador, was the venue for the Latin America Consultation on Holistic Ministry, held in November 1996. Twenty-four practitioners, reflectors and other participants attended the consultation. They came from 12 countries. Throughout the week, all who gathered at Quito engaged intensely in discussing the issues raised by the case studies. For some, the trip to Ecuador was the first time they traveled out of their native country. Meeting colleagues from other countries who shared the same vision was fascinating to them. It was not only beneficial to them personally but also necessary professionally to exchange views and experiences. In the work of the kingdom, we need more opportunities for professional interaction.

About this book

The format of this book is similar to earlier books in the series. Case studies and reflection chapters constitute the main body. The

1

cases selected for this book are some of the more fruitful ones that illustrate how holistic ministries are executed in Latin America. They are replete with lessons.

Alva Couto provides us with some of the contexts that holistic ministry practitioners encounter in Latin America and in which holistic ministry must be conducted. C. René Padilla's missiological-theological reflection will help advance the inquiry into effective holistic ministry one step further. Javier Mayorga shows us how we can analyze the cases from the perspective of strategic management. Bryant Myers guided the participants of the consultation in profiling the "ideal holistic practitioner." His chapter will be a valuable guide for identifying and training future holistic practitioners. In his conclusion, Myers skillfully pieces together some of the key issues expressed in this book.

Relationship to "symbiotic ministry"

In my earlier writings, I used the phrase "symbiotic ministry" to define the relationship between evangelism and social action. Since the appearance of *Serving with the Poor in Asia*, people knowledgeable of my earlier publications have asked me why I now use a different phraseology—a fair question which merits a comment from me.

I coined the phrase in 1976 to show my divergence from the concept of holistic ministry in vogue at that time. A big debate was going on within the world church in the 1960s, the 1970s, and the early 1980s related to evangelism vs. social action. The point I was making then was important to combat the eclecticism of the day, which emphasized evangelism over social action (as in the case of the evangelicals) and social action over evangelism (as in the case of denominations belonging to the World Council of Churches). There were obviously some notable exceptions in both camps. An excellent document, known as the Lausanne Covenant, was produced at the Lausanne Congress for World Evangelization in 1974. The World Council of Churches at its Nairobi Assembly in 1975 attempted to make a corresponding statement regarding what it considered to be evangelism and social action.

2

Holistic ministry in the past has often been associated with the lifting of one dimension of the church's concern (peace, social justice, poverty, human rights, or environment) over the others, and without connecting it to *missio Dei*. Publications on the subject were found wanting in their clear delineation of the *indispensability* of evangelism.

"Symbiosis" draws an analogy from the field of biology, "holism" from that of philosophy. Holistic ministry is a good phrase to use, if it considers evangelistic efforts to be an indispensable part of the church's vital ministry. Today's and tomorrow's mission contexts demand embodying our strategy in the concept of a true holistic ministry.

Need for further research

It is true that there have been consultations on holistic ministry before which have helped elevate the visibility of the concept of holism, but again, with little mention of the vital and necessary relationship of holism to evangelism. Something more was needed: to document examples of *effective* holistic ministry based on *empirical data* rather than plans and hopes.

This means two sets of investigations are necessary. We must collect actual cases of effective holistic ministry to test the hypotheses that: (1) relief and development, carefully executed holistically, lead to redemption; and (2) redemption, carefully nurtured holistically, leads to relief and development (compassionate acts). We can further subdivide these two main categories into six typological models:

> 1. Relief leads to redemption where there is a significant indigenous Christian movement (Example: the 1982 famine in Poland).
>
> 2. Relief leads to redemption where there is no significant indigenous Christian movement (Example: Cambodian refugees at Khao-I-Dang in 1979-80).
>
> 3. Development leads to redemption where there is a significant Christian movement (Example: Lake Mburo, Uganda).

4. Development leads to redemption where there is no significant Christian movement (Example: Juntavi in Bolivia).

5. Redemption leads to relief and development (compassionate acts) with outside intervention (Example: the China mission of the 1930s).

6. Redemption leads to relief and development (compassionate acts) without outside intervention (Example: Protestant "autonomous communities" in China after 1979).

With many such cases from various cultures under different circumstances, we can eventually formulate theories of holistic ministry, giving limitations and opportunities that relief and development organizations committed to doing effective holistic ministry may use. Not every holistic ministry attempt succeeds; we need to find out why. We have just begun to scratch the surface of what is to be a long and arduous search for truths in effective holistic ministry and about what God is doing at the frontier of world mission today.

It was this desire that led me to undertake the current series of holistic ministry consultations. With Howard Ahmanson and Steve Ferguson of Fieldstead promising a substantial multi-year grant, I formed a steering committee for the consultations. To discover the appropriate cases, I had to have the cooperation and participation of as many evangelical relief and development organizations as possible.

The consultation procedure

The current series of consultations focuses on case studies of development work leading to the formation of Christ groups. We have held consultations in Chiang Mai, Thailand, for Asia; in Harare, Zimbabwe, for Africa; and in Quito, Ecuador, for Latin America. For each consultation, we followed the same steps.

1. Call for summaries of case studies that demonstrate effective holistic ministry. Guidelines were

provided for the writing of such a case summary.

2. Selection of cases by the steering committee. Once chosen, the writers were asked to expand their summaries into papers.

3. Case study writers assembled for a one-week consultation to interact with reflectors on their papers. These reflectors are specialists in such fields as theology, sociology, anthropology, mission strategy, management, missiology, leadership development, modernity, and development theory.

4. Revision of papers, as needed, after the consultation.

5. Editing case studies and reflection papers for the book.

Latin American Christianity: Facts and features

Five centuries have passed since the arrival of Christopher Columbus on a Caribbean island. By 1900, the entire population of Latin America was considered Catholic, and a little less than 80 percent of almost half a billion people remain so today.

Evangelicals in Latin America have shown remarkable growth from a quarter of a million in 1900 to 46 million in 1990. Today, over 11 percent of Latin Americans are evangelicals. Even more remarkable has been the astonishing growth of the Pentecostal and charismatic churches. These churches have been successful in reaching the people who migrated to the cities from rural areas, thus constituting another layer of the urban poor.

The gap between the rich and the poor in Latin America is big and growing bigger—between the small group of upper classes and economic elites on the one hand, and the masses of slum dwellers and the rural poor on the other. Churches committed to the Great Commission must address the issue of poverty. It is in the midst of poverty that we find receptive people who stand in need of the gospel while they struggle to maintain their livelihood. Those who suffer in the midst of debilitating poverty may experi-

5

ence a credible witness to the power of the gospel when they come into contact with holistic practitioners living among them. Latin America needs a *liberating* theology which lifts Christ as the Liberator standing with open arms of welcome before the masses of nominal Christians who are enslaved to secular impact, poverty and spiritual impediments.

Approaches to nominal Christians

In Latin American countries, the influence of Catholicism has been so pervasive that many consider their country to be "Christian" and many, if not all, have been baptized in infancy. In "post-Christian" Europe, many of those baptized in state churches regard themselves neither as belonging to the church nor as being Christian. We must consider such "nominal" Christians everywhere, whether in Europe or in Latin America, to be in need of the gospel. Recognizing the presence of a large number of nominal Christians, Latin American churches of all denominations are involved in reviving and renewing their inactive members. Some among them have opted to start new churches rather than to revive or nurture inactive members.

We often encounter questions that essentially raise the same issue: Why should we attempt to reach those who are already Christians? The position of this consultation is that *lapsed* Christians must come into a living relationship with Christ in a Christ group that is alive and God-honoring. Indeed, everyone without Christ is lost and is in need of salvation. Salvation is to be found only in Christ, not in syncretistic and pagan practices. Further, the mission of Christ's church is to proclaim the gospel to every person.

Acknowledgments

I express my heartfelt thanks to Greg Rake, who has ably served as our consultation coordinator for Latin America. At the time I asked him to serve in this capacity, he was MAP International's Latin America director based in Quito. In the meantime, he received a call to join the staff of the Mennonite Board of Missions headquartered in Indiana, U.S.A. He was under tremendous pressure to wrap up his work at MAP and to become acclimated to his new post. Yet, his commitment to this consultation was such that he wanted to continue his assignment with us. I salute him.

We owe a debt of gratitude to Greg's successor, Mauricio Solís, and his staff in Quito for warmly welcoming us and serving as our able logistics team. They devoted their talents and countless hours to the success of the consultation. The team members are Jimena Perez, Lorena Estrella and Jim Oehrig, under the leadership of Mauricio Solís.

The members of the steering committee function as my advisors in executing this series of consultations. Each member is a busy person, and yet none of them hesitated to help when asked. I thank the members of the committee: Steve Ferguson of Fieldstead, Don Stephens of Mercy Ships, Bryant Myers of World Vision International and David Bussau of the Maranatha Trust. Milly Lugo of Fieldstead served as secretary of the committee and represented Fieldstead at the consultation with Don and Diana Schmierer. My special words of appreciation go to Don and Diana who, from the beginning of this series, have been enthusiastic supporters and encouragers. They have been present at every consultation.

Ken Ekström and Dave Evans of Food for the Hungry International were on hand for this consultation to assist the case study presenters in finalizing their writing. Both men are conversant in English and Spanish. They also took turns in serving as translators, as did Jim Oehrig of MAP-Latin America.

John Kenyon and his staff at MARC are true professionals. Their production of this book, as before, is of quality and no doubt the readers would give it high marks.

To all these and others not mentioned, I offer my thanks.

Part one

Case Studies

1

The Evangelical Hospital, Honduras

Enrique Martínez

The Evangelical Hospital was founded in 1949 in Siguate-peque, a town located in the central region of Honduras. It was begun by the Central American Mission (CAM International), and in 1969 passed to Honduran hands, becoming an autonomous national organization that is a member of the Association of Central American Churches.

The Evangelical Hospital is a private, not-for-profit, self-sustaining entity, under a national organization, the Association of Evangelical Hospitals. This association is comprised of Christian leaders from various churches and from different professional backgrounds. The association in turn names a board of directors in charge of administrating the hospital. Internally there is an administrative committee composed of the heads of the different sections of the hospital. This committee assists the director with his executive mandate.

HISTORICAL CONTEXT

When the Evangelical Hospital project began in 1949, Honduras was a predominantly rural nation—approximately 70 percent of the population was located in rural areas. It was extremely poor and its

11

economy was highly dependent on banana production, which was controlled by multinational firms.

The lack of an adequate system of roads and communication practically divided the nation in two: the Atlantic coastal area to the north and the interior mountainous region. Health care was deficient and in many areas of the country nonexistent.

Roman Catholicism was a dominant force in the nation's life; it was conservative, had a great deal of nominalism, and was syncretistic in practice. The evangelical church, although present, was a minority with little influence on national life.

Faced with these circumstances and considering its strategic location between the two most important cities of Honduras, Siguatepeque was chosen as the hospital site. At that time, Siguatepeque was an agricultural and forestry town with fewer than four thousand inhabitants. It was a halfway point for road travelers going between Tegucigalpa and San Pedro Sula, a trip that used to take approximately twelve hours.

Almost simultaneously with the establishment of the Evangelical Hospital, missionary pilots for "Wings of Mercy" (of Mission Aviation Fellowship) began to fly in Honduras, establishing a base and landing field on land near the hospital. With this air service, it became possible to transport people from remote and isolated areas throughout the country for medical attention at the hospital.

There have been some changes in the last 47 years. Honduras is still a poor and dependent nation with a population of 5 million, unmanageable foreign debt and a deteriorating quality of life. The evangelical church has grown to include almost 20 percent of the population. Communications have improved, and access to the hospital by land is easy from different parts of the country.

Siguatepeque has improved its situation and now has a population of approximately 40,000 people. It is the most important vegetable-growing region in Honduras and has also been turned into a coffee-growing region. Its location has made the area one of significant commercial activity. It boasts the most developed horticultural cooperative in the nation, and is seat to the National Forestry School and to various development agencies.

MINISTRY DESCRIPTION

Characteristics of the ministry

From the beginning, the project has had several distinguishing characteristics.

a) *Explicit goal of self-management and sustainability.* In 1962, the Central American Mission specified the following goal for its institutions, which it added to its constitution: "The boards of directors for the institutions shall include dedicated national believers as soon as feasible, with the goal that with time these boards will come to be completely national, providing their own means, leaders and personnel."

This purpose was clearly assimilated and assumed by Dr. Marion McKinney, founder of the hospital, who from the beginning worked to create the conditions necessary for this process. In the early sixties McKinney wrote: "Given that it is desirable and necessary that the Evangelical Hospital work towards the goal of being a completely national institution, we have reflected on some of the requisites to achieving this purpose. It is obvious that it cannot be attained in the blink of an eye. Rather it has to be the fruit of years of study and progressive change until it becomes a firmly based reality . . ." In 1969, the management of the hospital was handed over to Honduran nationals. The hospital had become self-sustaining several years before this, so that at the time of transfer the mission was only providing the salaries of the last foreign missionaries.

b) *Discipleship.* To fulfill the goal of self-management, there has always been a great emphasis on teaching. McKinney again: "The Hondurans need to become aware of the need to prepare themselves for assuming the great responsibility which will be theirs in the not so distant future. It should be a challenge for the people of the gospel to inspire the youth to prepare themselves to be continuously occupying posts of responsibility in the future not only in institutions but also in other fields of the Lord's work. In order that the hospital may continually function in an appropriate manner, always as a positive testimony of the gospel, it is necessary that all positions in the board of directors and administrative committee be

13

occupied always by people who are dedicated to the Lord, who recognize and consider the hospital as property and work of the Lord. The life, health, functioning, testimony and survival of the project depend on the dedication of its members."

It is noteworthy that this vision has borne fruit; the hospital has progressively transformed itself without losing the core of its mission and commitment to Jesus Christ.

c) *Simple work style.* The hospital work style has tried to balance various aspects such as functionality and cleanliness with sobriety and a rejection of ostentation. The buildings were built from stone obtained from a quarry on hospital property and most of its furnishings were made from wood obtained locally. Generally speaking, medical equipment is purchased used and is well maintained.

d) *Coordination with the Ministry of Health.* When the hospital opened there were no medical services in Siguatepeque and outlying areas. It was not until the sixties and seventies that the Honduran Ministry of Health implemented a more structured system throughout the country. The hospital cooperates closely with the Ministry of Health in certain areas, such as immunization, training and as requested by the Ministry.

e) *Teaching.* From 1958-68 the hospital operated a professional nursing school. In 1971 a training center for nurse's aids and laboratory and x-ray technicians began operation; the students graduate with a diploma that is recognized by the Ministry of Health.

f) *Cooperation with other organizations and churches.* The hospital ministry has participated in joint activities with other Christian institutions as well as local churches of different denominations.

g) *Service to the dispossessed.* A consisted effort is made to reach people with few economic resources, as expressed by McKinney: "Medical services should be offered to the poor at the lowest possible price within the limits of maintaining economic solvency." This has not been easy because of the self-sustaining character of hospital services, but some mechanisms have been created to achieve this objective.

Hospital services

a) *Medical attention.* There is a staff of medical personnel geared toward general medicine with an emphasis on surgery. In addition, there are consulting specialists from Tegucigalpa and San Pedro Sula that offer their services.

The hospital has a dental clinic, laboratory, complete clinic, x-rays, ultrasound, endoscopy, electrocardiography and other support services. It has two operating rooms and a delivery room, an area for hospitalization (66 beds), with general wards, semiprivate and private rooms, and rooms for pediatric and maternity patients.

b) *Pastoral services.* From the beginning there has been an evangelistic emphasis as part of the Christian lifestyle of hospital staff. Work is also done in counseling, consolation and biblical reflection for patients and staff.

c) *Teaching.* 1) A training center for nurse's aids and laboratory and x-ray technicians; 2) continuing medical education to keep medical staff abreast of the latest developments; 3) in-service education—a program to keep nursing and laboratory staff current.

d) *Community services* include: 1) Primary health care in a community clinic located in the town of El Porvenir; 2) support for churches and Christian organizations in the areas of holistic health, social responsibility, health education and ecology; 3) document center; 4) health promotion in the community; 5) support of a training center in community matters; 6) special programs for high-risk health groups (high blood pressure, obesity, diabetes, smokers), and on sexuality and AIDS; 7) networks for holistic health; and 8) a radio program called "Our Health."

SPIRITUAL IMPACT

The ministry's spiritual impact has been extensive. A quantitative index to which most missionary agencies assign much importance is the number of professions of faith. If we take this as a reference point, the ministry has registered approximately 14,000 professions of faith.

Nevertheless, considering that quantitative data are not always adequate, some aspects that can more truly reveal the impact that the Evangelical Hospital ministry has had in spiritual matters and in the mission of the church are listed here.

1. *Lives that have been authentically transformed* with fruit for all to see. There are many cases, with a long period of follow-up, of people whose lives have been transformed by the Lord through the hospital's ministry. One example of a transformed life is the current president of the board of directors.

2. *The development of congregations.* Through the hospital's direct and indirect efforts, various congregations have grown. Historically, the Betel Church has been particularly associated with the hospital, because it was founded with the direct support of members of this ministry and of Wings of Mercy. A large number of hospital staff actively participate in this local church, which has been a model for the search for holistic integration in missionary work.

3. *Spiritual influence in the community.* In 1929, missionary Anna Thomas wrote: "Work in Siguatepeque is difficult and requires much patience. . . . Undoubtedly it is one of the most indifferent fields in Honduras. Drunkenness and immorality prevail . . ."

   Today Siguatepeque is one of the towns in Honduras with the largest percentage of evangelical Christians (about 40 percent), and has been influenced by Christian values in its social life. Several Christians have participated in community sociopolitical activities.

4. *Support and facilitation of other Christian ministries.* As a pioneering ministry in Honduras, the hospital has always been ready to cooperate in the development of other Christian ministries, among them: Evangelical educational institutions, the Central American Bible Institute of Honduras (IBCAH), Latin American Theological Brotherhood (FTL), Christian Medical Association of Honduras, the Honduras Biblical Association, and the Evangelical Educational Community.

5. *Collaboration through networks.* From its founding, when it worked closely with Wings of Mercy, the hospital has contin-

ued developing coordinated activities with like-minded organizations, such as those mentioned above and others including Bible societies, KNH-Honduras, Christian Health Association (ACSA), CONSEDE and the Honduras Evangelical Fellowship.

In 1992 an agreement of cooperation with MAP International (Latin American office) was signed to provide a greater and more comprehensive community services program, and in general to strengthen the hospital ministry. Through the hospital's community services program, agreements have been signed to develop training programs with EIRENE International and the Center for Interdisciplinary Studies in Theology (CETI) of the Kairos Community.

The hospital maintains close ties of cooperation with the Honduras Bible Institute to develop health and agricultural modules for students in the program of ministerial training, in which leaders of rural churches participate. Without having to leave home, the students periodically receive four modules per year.

6. *Support of local churches.* The hospital has directly supported local churches with aid and through its program of community services. An indirect and valuable contribution has also been providing human resources for the various local churches.

7. *Contributions to processes of transformation and biblical reflection.* With the contacts it has acquired over the years, the hospital has played a leading role in processes of transformation and biblical reflection. It has enjoyed the contributions of renowned Christian leaders and theologians such as Emilio Antonio Nuñez, C. René Padilla, Juan Stam, Pedro Puigvert, David Lacueva, Evis Carballosa, David Suazo, Paul Clark, Eduardo Ramirez, Stanley Slade, Israel Ortiz, Esly Carvalho, Helen Pratt, Abel Morales and others that have enriched reflection and church activities in general. There has also been cooperation on this issue with diverse organizations such as the Latin American Theological Community, EIRENE

International, MAP International, World Vision, Latin American Christian Medical Association (AMCLA), Bible societies, Bible Union (Association), Christian Health Association (ACSA) and KNH.

SOCIAL IMPACT

On persons directly related with hospital work

* *Employment.* The hospital is one of the larger employers in Siguatepeque. More than 100 people work at the hospital and a significant additional number at occasional jobs.
* *Decent working conditions.* Hospital policy is to provide decent working conditions in accordance with the law, and strives for better alternatives.
* *Better living conditions for families of employees.* A savings and loan association for employees has been organized, along with a commissary of basic items.

In the community

1. *Economic contributions that benefit the community.*
   * Direct: Through taxes paid to the municipal government (despite its status as a not-for-profit entity), and various purchases that benefit suppliers.
   * Indirect: Community income due to the large number of patients that come from other regions and pay for lodging, food, transportation and other services, thus benefitting the community.
2. *Extension work in different community projects.*

Within Honduras

* *Attention and aid* with the offer of a model of alternative assistance that has served people in all parts of the country.
* *Contributions to the national health system through the training of qualified personnel.* While the nursing school was in operation, 60 nurses received training and are now working in different parts of the country. One of the alumni is now director of the first graduate program for nurses in Honduras. Over two

hundred nurse's aides and 56 lab technicians have graduated from the hospital's training center.

In the words of founder Dr. Marion McKinney, the hospital was "dedicated to God for the good of the Honduran people, with the hope that each patient would find not only health in body, but also salvation of [their] soul . . ."

We can mention from the standpoint of holistic ministry the initial limitations and achievements in relation to the historical moment. In the forties and fifties, the missionary movement originating in the United States emphasized almost exclusively the proclamatory aspect of evangelism. It was a time of much hostility to the preaching of the gospel and it became evident that social works, including medical attention, were a medium for reaching people who otherwise would not have contact with evangelical sectors. We should note that these health care services were a manifestation of compassion for the health needs of the Honduran people, and as important as the work of evangelization. Altruism and excellence were evident in patient care.

Other relevant aspects should be noted.

a) *The process of transferring control from foreign missionaries to national missionaries.* Dr. McKinney and others made outstanding efforts in the training and preparation of teams that would take on hospital management, teams that included people who would later serve on the board of directors, the medical staff, nursing staff and others. As with all transitions there were problems, but the transfer eventually brought renewal and a more contextualized perspective.

b) *National workers committed to missionary work.* A sense of service and mission have been intertwined. The entire hospital staff is involved in the task, which is why it is not uncommon to find doctors, nurses, administrative personnel and others involved in sharing the gospel, and chaplains helping out in community areas.

c) *Sustainability.* For over 25 years, the hospital has been a self-sustaining organization through the medical services it provides. It should be noted that compared to private hospitals, costs for ser-

19

vices at the hospital are significantly less. Despite this, there are many extremely poor people who cannot pay these lower costs. For their benefit a special fund—the "Good Samaritan"—has been created, which is maintained by personal and institutional contributions from national and international sources.

d) *Training.* From the start, training has been stressed. Because of this emphasis, the hospital has provided health care personnel that are now working in different areas of the country and in other nations as well.

e) *Recognition.* The hospital is known nationally and internationally as an organization that is managed with integrity. There is an annual audit, and individuals and organizations that have made contributions are informed of the use of their funds. This has created influence among churches, Christian organizations and government authorities.

CHALLENGES

The hospital faces several challenges for the future. Among them are: continual renewal without losing sight of its fundamental commitment to the Lord's kingdom and to justice; providing high-quality, low-cost medical attention; maintaining self-financing and obtaining necessary funds for special projects; and enhancing training programs. The hospital must continue to facilitate holistic health and be a living example of Christian service.

2

Grassroots, church-based development in Honduras

Alexis Andino

The experiences of a group of eight rural churches in the southern Honduran province of Choluteca demonstrate the benefits of collaboration between a Christian nongovernmental organization and local churches. In approximately three years (1992-95), these churches have helped organize and train local community development leaders, coordinated various community development efforts, reached out to other communities and seen three new churches planted and aggregate church participation double.

The current process began with the involvement of CEDEN (*Comité Evangélico de Desarrollo y Emergencia Nacional*—the National Evangelical Development and Emergency Committee), a national nongovernmental organization founded by a number of evangelical denominations in the early 1970s. CEDEN staff began training eight rural pastors during a period of approximately 10 months. This training focused on the role of the church in the community in the areas of evangelization and social action.

Over the years this process led to the founding of a grassroots development organization called CORCRIDE (*Comité Regional Cris-*

tiano de Desarrollo—the Regional Christian Committee for Development). This group is made up of pastors and lay leaders from local churches in 11 communities in the region of El Triunfo, Choluteca. These people are the official representatives of the local churches, which represent five different denominations.

THE CONTEXT

The region has a high level of poverty. The people are engaged mainly in agriculture, and may also be involved in commercial and salaried work through emerging businesses that are dedicated to exploiting marine life (e.g., shrimp).

Some of the problems identified by the leadership of CORCRIDE include malnutrition, low agricultural production, low levels of education, less rainfall due to deforestation, soil degradation, lack of respect for the environment, contaminated water, lack of cleanliness in the homes, family disintegration, alcoholism and drug abuse and immorality.

Local resources include ample human resources, community and church leaders, land (though there are some problems with land tenure), sources of water, fertile soil in many places and adequate rainfall.

At the beginning of the process of reflection, training and practice in community development, much of the population claimed to be Roman Catholic, but mostly in a nominal way. Many of the people that today are heavily involved with the development processes that CORCRIDE facilitates used to participate in Catholic religious services.

THE FORMATION OF CORCRIDE

CORCRIDE's purpose is to strengthen the ministry of the local churches in the area of Christian service, initially in the municipalities of El Triunfo, El Corpus, Concepción de María and Namasigue, which are all located in the province of Choluteca.

I joined CEDEN in February 1991. For me it was a dream come true because, after having worked in community development for six years, I wanted to join the institution that in Honduras has historically been the pioneer among Christian service institutions. I had been involved with CEDEN through my work with World Relief in Honduras in 1985-87.

Toward the end of 1990 CEDEN decided to change its focus from a development model with a high degree of paternalism to one that was more participative and contextual. On my first day at this institution, I joined a group of about 20 brothers and sisters from 10 member agencies of CONSEDE (*Consejo de Instituciones Evangélicas de Desarrollo*—the Council of Evangelical Development Institutions, of which CEDEN has been a member for many years). My personal commitment and challenge at that time were to honor the opportunity that God had given me to take part in and to learn from the "CEDEN school," as many of us called it.

I moved to Choluteca to coordinate the southern region for CEDEN in April 1990—a formidable challenge, according to my teammates from Tegucigalpa. The work with the communities there and especially with the regional team was difficult due to the history of the program in this region.

CEDEN had been working in the Choluteca region for about 10 years. During that time CEDEN—which had been founded by the leading evangelical denominations in Honduras—and the local churches had gradually grown apart. Some of the churches were so opposed to Christian involvement in development work that they disciplined their members who became involved with CEDEN's work. CEDEN's regional office and the local churches had started working independently from each other until they distanced themselves to such a degree that even the informal relationship between the church and CEDEN's local employees was lost. That is the situation I faced when I moved to Choluteca.

Several of us regional staff members began building personal relationships with a small group of pastors from five (later eight) local churches. The denominations represented by these pastors included Central American Mission, Assemblies of God, Baptist and the Interdenominational Mission Church. This group of pastors—years later they would form CORCRIDE—began their work together in 1991 with the technical and training support of CEDEN.

23

After this initial training of pastors, laypersons were involved—first one deacon chosen by each church, and then five community leaders chosen by each community. These community leaders (or promoters) included two midwives, one health promoter, one agricultural promoter and one preschool teacher from each community. CEDEN facilitated bringing in outside technical staff to train these community leaders who, in turn, taught their neighbors. Some material inputs in the areas of health and agriculture were also provided.

Unfortunately, CEDEN went through a major shakeup at this time and disappeared from the scene. I left CEDEN in September 1993, and after CEDEN left the area I maintained permanent contact with the group of pastors. For about a year I and two Christian brothers took the time to visit the group every month to carry out training activities. Out of this process the idea arose in the participants' minds to form a board of directors to formalize their efforts to help the communities. This process culminated in August 1994 with the group's decision to incorporate as a nonprofit organization called CORCRIDE.

RECENT HISTORY OF CORCRIDE

Since August 1994, CORCRIDE has:

❖ continued the leadership training process;
❖ carried out diagnostic studies in each community;
❖ expanded the number of deacons involved from one to two per church; and
❖ incorporated the pastors and deacons into the community development team of trained leaders in each community (the pastors serve as liaisons between the community-level teams and CORCRIDE).

These community-based community development teams have:

❖ worked on projects to improve the access roads to the communities;
❖ developed a project to build ovens for baking bread;
❖ promoted latrine and home improvements;

- ❖ promoted family gardens; and
- ❖ organized groups to clean yards and roads.

CORCRIDE had organized itself so well that in 1995 it received a small grant from Christian Reformed World Relief Committee (CRWRC) to train their board of directors and to allow them to obtain legal status as a nonprofit organization.

RESULTS

The impact of CORCRIDE's work can be seen in the leadership and credibility that the local evangelical churches enjoy in the eyes of the local communities and authorities. It can also be perceived in the work of more than 20 volunteers who constantly work to encourage and train individuals from the local churches and communities.

Since 1992 three new congregations have been formed, bringing the number of churches involved in CORCRIDE to 11. In addition, the existing churches have experienced strong growth. The total attendance in the churches involved has increased from approximately 500 in 1992 to 1,000 in 1995, representing over 12 percent of the aggregate population of the communities involved (this does not include data from other evangelical churches in these same communities that are not directly involved in CORCRIDE). This represents an annual growth rate of 20-26 percent, depending on whether one begins the calculation from the beginning or the end of the period of the pastors' training. Migration due to regional unemployment has reduced church growth figures as believers move elsewhere.

In comparison, Patrick Johnstone (*Operation World*, Grand Rapids: Zondervan, 1993) estimates that "Protestants" (evangelicals in Latin American parlance) in Honduras overall were growing at a rate of 6 percent, and represented 11 percent of the population.

As mentioned above, the impact on the other evangelical churches has not been quantified. Even harder to measure is the impact on the Roman Catholic churches, although at least a couple of Delegates of the Word (Catholic lay ministers) are involved in the process as community leaders.

25

In some communities where the work has been going on for several years, we have observed that the relationships between families have improved, and there is greater and more frequent participation in community activities by community members. The members of these communities have worked together on projects such as latrine repair, repairing access roads and supporting informal preschool programs.

For example, in 1994 CORCRIDE encouraged three communities to use their own resources to repair some 30 latrines that had fallen into disrepair. This involved a process of reviewing with the people the importance of using latrines. In Bijagual about eight new latrines were built using fiber-concrete slabs provided by the Ministry of Health.

Also in 1994, CORCRIDE assisted the community of Palo de Agua with the repair of its three kilometer access road. This process was repeated in 1995 after the rainy season was over.

In 1995 CORCRIDE encouraged and organized the women in three communities who had been trained as bakers to build two beehive-type ovens in each community. The ovens have allowed these women to bake and sell bread either as individuals or, as in the case of one group of women in Matapalos, to develop a group-based microenterprise.

In 1995-96 CORCRIDE obtained some donated vegetable seeds from the Ministry of Agriculture, which have been planted by several families in each community. In 1996 CORCRIDE also bought some vegetable seeds with funds from the CRWRC.

It is very clear that a process of integral transformation has begun in this area. Although it will have the same limitations that all processes of this type have, it has demonstrated that one does not need great quantities of money to be part of the work of evangelization and social ministry among the needy. In the case of CORCRIDE, the initial investment is not known to the penny, but we know that whatever the amount was, it was well spent considering the changes we have witnessed in the area.

This process also calls us to reflect on whether we can already talk about an integral transformation or realize that we have to be patient and recognize that today we plant the seeds, but we should not expect to be the ones who bring in the harvest tomorrow, because it is more likely that those who come after us will be the ones to do so.

HOW PEOPLE HAVE COME TO KNOW CHRIST

Many of the people who have accepted the Lord have in one way or another carried out community work in response to CORCRIDE's efforts. Today, through the relationships that have been built, many have made the most important decision of their lives. Indeed, three new churches have been "raised up" by incorporating new believers.

Three of the leaders involved with the process have identified several factors that have contributed to church growth.

- Direct involvement of the church in social work.
- The organization of the pastors and deacons (and church committees in certain communities).
- The visible unity of the body of Christ as the churches work side-by-side.
- Relationships have dissolved the wall of fear that existed between nonevangelicals and evangelicals.
- More transparency on the part of the evangelical churches.
- Devotional times in community meetings.
- CORCRIDE's promotion of community participation.

CONCEPTUALIZING OUR MISSION

I became involved in the strengthening of the pastors of the local churches not as a job but because I have the conviction that God calls each Christian to carry out the Great Commission through discipling and teaching. All of this requires passion to serve our fellow human beings. We are called to preach a holistic gospel where, besides attending to people's "spiritual" needs, we must also be concerned about their "physical" needs, just as our Lord Jesus Christ modeled for us.

Based on these experiences, I wish to share some principles of local church-based transformation and development that I have

27

noticed were put to use by Christians in the southern part of Honduras.

- ❖ A conviction to serve the Lord.
- ❖ The desire to learn.
- ❖ Exposing our lives and knowledge to others.
- ❖ Not considering oneself unique or "chosen," but as a useful tool in the expansion of the Kingdom of God.
- ❖ The need to respect, value and support the local authorities, in whatever way is biblically acceptable.

EVALUATION

This is a case in which a Christian nongovernmental organization denied itself, ceding the control of the process into the hands of the community members—something which has been very rare in Honduras. This was both intentional on the part of the CEDEN staff involved and circumstantial (or providential) due to CEDEN's internal crisis.

A key factor was the attitude of the leaders in developing a vision for their communities, and their willingness to move ahead even when they received no institutional support. Another positive factor was that the group that became CORCRIDE began with essentially no financial resources. This forced them to identify their own potential and concentrate on the development of human resources.

A difficulty has been the mostly seasonal migration of community members and the weakening effect this has had on the church during certain times of the year. Another negative factor is the pressure that some political parties have put on certain leaders involved with CORCRIDE to become involved in local politics, especially as the political parties are looking for candidates for the 1997 elections. This could compromise CORCRIDE's work if their roles become confused in the eyes of the community.

The members of this group have become my friends, teachers and models of personal commitment to the kingdom of God. There are more lessons in this process that I have not been able to document here. My first obligation is to God, because I am grateful for the gift of my life on earth and for the eternal life God has given me. My second obligation is to my friends from El Triunfo, because I have learned so much from them. There is still hope in the midst of the economic and moral poverty in our communities. We must see a great potential for the transformation of those who live there.

3
The Redeemer Project, Brazil

Claudio Oliver

THE CONTEXT

The Redeemer Project has been working with street people, adolescents and battered women in the city of Curitiba since 1993. Curitiba has a population of 1.5 million inhabitants and is the capital of the southern Brazilian state of Paraná. Its people come from many ethnic groups, the majority of whom have European roots.

Although it has the highest quality of life among Brazil's large cities, there is a rapidly growing class of poor and disenfranchised people who live on the streets. The city tends to be egocentric and has an unofficial policy of hiding this underclass and painting over the consequences of their poverty. That said, the social programs available to the poor are better than in many other Brazilian cities.

The city has many evangelical churches of various denominations, with high growth rates among the middle class. In general, these churches are neither involved in social action nor in speaking out against the injustice perpetrated on the poor.

The Redeemer Project works with four major groups of poor people: street people, the unemployed, adolescents and battered women.

Street people

The project has identified three groups of street people in Curitiba. The first are victims of personal or collective calamity (1 Kings 17, Job) that find themselves in a desperate situation. The second group consists of people exploited either by the socioeconomic system or by other people (Amos 4:1), and so are blocked from access to society and lack the dignity that is rooted in being created in the image of God. The third group consists of people who are victims of their own pride or laziness (Proverbs 21:25), and other vices that deceive and enslave.

In comparison to Curitiba's white majority, the street people are primarily of mixed-race origins (white, black and native Brazilian). These people are victims of a system of social "apartheid" that Brazilian society practices. This system views black, indigenous and white poor people as human possessions that exist merely to serve as fuel for the furnace that powers one of the world's largest economies, and surely one of the most unjust.

In this setting the elite behave with total disdain by hanging on to a social system that has not changed significantly in almost five centuries. Despite the existence of social change and improvement, instead of helping the poor acquire a situation of dignity the elite only help them to survive and thereby better serve their masters. This situation provokes the wrath of God (Ezekiel 16:49-50, Isaiah 5:8), and has led project participants to speak out against injustice.

The street people belong to three main religious groups: traditional (primarily Roman Catholic) and evangelical Christianity, the Afro-Brazilian religions and agnosticism with tendencies toward alternative cultures.

The unemployed

Brazil's adoption of a neoconservative economic model has resulted in fewer available opportunities in the labor market, forcing a growing number of people to live on the streets. In addition, an increased concentration of wealth and land into the hands of fewer people has led to a substantial population movement from rural areas as people search for employment in the cities.

Most of these people have inadequate schooling, no technical training and have begun a life of personal disintegration due to a lack of orientation and guidance. Many have learned to survive in this hostile environment through petty crime, theft, cheating and lying. The majority of the unemployed with whom the project works come from a rural Catholic tradition, and a small percentage from Pentecostalism.

Adolescents

The third group that the project works with is adolescents at risk. These are young people of low income who have recently been released from Christian halfway houses and are at risk of becoming involved in street crime. Due to the years spent in Christian institutions, these adolescents have some knowledge of the gospel, but have not had a real conversion experience.

Battered women

These are poor women who live temporarily in a municipal institution created to protect them from domestic violence. The average stay there is three months. During this period, the municipality helps the women to find work so they can achieve a certain level of economic independence. Almost all of these women are nominal Catholics or involved with Afro-Brazilian spiritism.

THE PROJECT'S VISION AND MISSION

The Redeemer Project is a parachurch organization made up of Christians from various churches and denominations. Our first priority and commitment is to proclaim the gospel of our Lord Jesus Christ. Coming to faith and repentance in light of this gospel is the only way that people can be truly free. We understand our great need of the power and anointing of the Holy Spirit to confront and triumph over the powers of this world, both visible and invisible. Our mission is to meet and serve Jesus Christ through the poorest of the poor in Curitiba. Our vision began with the realization that we are sinners—individually and corporately—and that we must repent of our sins and be obedient to the call of Jesus in Matthew 25:31-46.

Our vision is rooted in the examples of the church's past, starting with Christ's ministry and drawing from the Acts of the Apostles, the early church fathers, the Christian mystics, the Reformation, pietism, evangelicalism and pentecostalism. In this way we try to remain firmly established in the reformed tradition, while at the same time drawing from the life of the church orders in the Middle Ages with their practices of meditation, prayer, silence and simple living.

When we began our ministry in 1993, we had no preconceived ideas about the people we were going to serve or what their problems were. We simply went out into the streets to meet Jesus, and that is exactly what happened. We were privileged to have the opportunity to touch the wounds of Jesus and we realized that we were the only possibility that the poor had to be touched by him, because we are his body on this earth (Matthew 25:40). In that way, the Jesus present in us met the Jesus present in the poor and both groups were changed by the encounter.

Out of this experience we decided first to practice our service to the poor and then to reflect on that service. Our practice taught us that good relationships and a spirit of service carried out in humility and simplicity were the keys to our ministry. We have discovered the importance of our relationship with and service to God, to each other in the project, to the poor and the church. Within the Redeemer Project, we believe that authority is a fundamental principle, but that it should be decentralized and horizontal. In addition, we view ourselves as a living organism instead of an organization, which allows for flexibility and the ability to adapt quickly to changing circumstances and needs. In keeping with our horizontal structure, we do not try to meet all the needs of the people we serve, but instead have learned to specialize in a few things and refer people to other institutions and the church for other needs.

Our outreach style is both creative and simple, so that we may present a concrete message that is easily grasped by those we serve. For example, we use skits, sleight of hand, footwashing and other alternative methods to get across the gospel message. A good team spirit project is very important to us and we get together often to share meals, have parties or just to be together. These gatherings are excellent ways to promote relationships and to maintain a positive attitude among the project members.

The Redeemer Project has four paid staff members and 35 volunteers. The volunteers form the backbone of the organism and perform most of the work. They are generally given simple tasks that can be accomplished quickly, thereby maintaining a high level of motivation and degree of satisfaction.

THE PROJECT'S HISTORY

The Redeemer Project began without the support of the community or the local churches, or even a well-structured plan. It came about simply as the result of the vision of a group of young people from a church in crisis that decided to come closer to Jesus in the spirit of Matthew 25, reaching out to people who are suffering and tending to their immediate need of food, hygiene and clothing.

In the beginning, the project used a church kitchen for the production and distribution of bread and hot chocolate to the poorest of the poor. As a result, these youth found themselves on the streets, identifying with the alcoholics and drug addicts. During these encounters, team members would try to approach the street people in a loving way and begin a process of friendship and trust. The team spent a long time just trying to get to know the street people until they felt that perhaps they might be able to offer them something more.

After a time, the team began to invite poor people to use the church's basement on Sunday mornings for baths, a change of clothes and a small worship service that used simple and accessible language based on the parables and the life of Jesus. This quickly began to produce positive results and some of the poor decided to enter rehabilitation homes for recovery. Due to some changes the church building was not being used for worship services, and the project began to use it as a temporary shelter for men who were getting ready to enter a rehabilitation program or who were beginning the process of trying to re-enter society.

Due to further changes the church building had to be vacated, and the project went to work to find a found a house for their ministry activities. The team found a house in a semi-abandoned state and worked together to restore it, supported by the local church and other Christians. This was a significant time for the team as we learned to work together. In addition, the team was maturing in its vision and manner of working with street people.

When the project reached that point, we sought out the city's mayor with the intention of offering our ministry as a means of cooperating with the established structures. After this meeting we continued to work as before, but with closer ties to the public hospitals that had services for alcohol and drug recovery. Several months later, city representatives came to us and asked us to coordinate a new city shelter that was to be inaugurated in a few months.

The team's initial reaction to this opportunity was that it would be an impossible task (Jeremiah 1:6), given our small administrative structure and limited personnel. After several meetings, however, we decided to take up the challenge. We told the city authorities that we would do it on the condition that we would hold daily worship services and a special breakfast on Sunday. Our conditions were accepted and we began to organize a group of churches that would cooperate with us in this initiative. We chose 50 volunteers and eight workers from among the members of the Evangelical Lutheran Church, the Salvation Army, the Agape Community, the Hermon Community and the Community of Christ.

After a training period, we began the work in conjunction with the municipality in the winter of 1995. The shelter includes municipal administration offices, roving health clinics, attention for the poor, a cafeteria, a kitchen, rooms for literacy classes and occupational therapy. The city shelter was run with the vision of redeeming life and offering professional treatment to the poor population in general, and specifically to the street people, in the hope that they would re-enter society. The shelter was open 24 hours a day, seven days a week, including holidays, with no restrictions on the kinds of people the shelter would offer services to.

This partnership with the public sector worked very well until the city authorities decided to alter the program and opt for the old system of trying to hide the city's "undesirables." As a result, they began to replace the original staff that had been involved with the initial task, dismantling and reorganizing the teams, and changing the methodology of attention and treatment that had been used up to that point. In the face of this situation and the realization that the new program would not promote life, we complained to the mayor. Unfortunately, there was no room for dialogue and the mayor's office terminated our involvement in the shelter.

This critical event provided the impetus we needed to take another step forward in our ministry. We moved back into our old house and started a living center where men and women received food, work referrals, documentation assistance, medical assistance, two daily Bible studies, guidance and counseling. Rather than becoming discouraged by our removal from involvement in the city shelter, we were motivated to regroup and move forward.

THE PROJECT'S MINISTRY

The Redeemer Project has three major ministry components: the Living Center, the Reintegration Home and street outreach.

The Living Center

Our main ministry is focused on the Living Center. Three employees and two interns serve the poor who come for baths, food, activities, interviews and two daily Bible studies. We try to maintain the center as a place of silence and prayer, an oasis in the midst of the agitation and violence of the streets. All of the activities begin and end with periods of silence, prayer and reflection. We have an average of 200 people a month that come to the center for attention.

In addition to the daily program, there are weekly interviews with a psychologist. We hope to introduce occupational therapy and music therapy as resources permit. We have also given space to two additional projects begun by people to whom we had ministered in the past. The first project, run by two individuals who were beggars, is a silk-screen workshop where people paint T-shirts and other items with their own tools. The second project is for adolescents who produce wrapping paper and special packaging for local stores with recycled paper.

In addition, the Living Center houses the state office of Narcotics Anonymous, which also has a group that meets five times a week at the center. We have signed an agreement with a commission of the Federal Social Bank to begin a job creation program. We have also signed an agreement with the Creativity Center of Curitiba (Secretary of Industry and Commerce) to place ten people in its arts and crafts training program. Later this year we hope to start an income-generating program based on the production and sale of ecologically sound products.

The Reintegration Home

We have some space at our Living Center that serves as a home for men who are coming out of the rehab programs and for adolescents who need to reintegrate into society. The home is our attempt to reduce the high relapse rates. In this program, they spend about a year with us during which they work to find a home church, get a job and, whenever possible, have their family life restored.

At this point, the program concentrates on teaching people to deal with freedom in a responsible manner. The guests must learn the rules of living and managing their time together in the home. In addition, we teach financial management based on Christian principles. Weekly self-help groups are run by a psychologist, an economic program strives to build a small savings account for them to use once they leave the home, and they are taught to deal with government bureaucracy.

Street outreach

Two groups are on the streets on a weekly basis to minister to the needs of the poor. We consider this to be a fundamental component in our attempt to maintain the simplicity and identity of our original calling. When we are on the streets a kind word, a piece of bread and an invitation to come and visit us have been the most effective methods to break the invisible barrier that keeps the street people imprisoned in the street underworld.

The Project's Impact

The Redeemer Project has had an impact on three groups of people: the poor, local churches and volunteers, and municipal staff.

The poor

There are several hundred street people who live in Curitiba, and all of them have been served at least once by the Redeemer Project. Several of these people have been converted through the project's ministry. We continue to be surprised by the number of former street people that we meet who are now in local churches, have jobs and are reintegrated into society. For example, the first man that we met on the streets is now part of—and a great blessing to—my local church. As a fruit of our labor at the city shelter, 39 people have returned to their families, several families who were in dire straits were referred by our partnership to municipal programs that have allowed them to have their own homes, and are now attending local churches. Some men have gone into rehab programs or hospitals in an effort to end their alcohol and drug abuse.

In addition, the Redeemer Project is well known in the city and on the streets, and street people use the project as a model against which to compare other similar programs. Many street people that were rejected by other programs because of their violent behavior have been welcomed at the project and have changed their conduct due to the relationships and environment of the Living Center. Street people know that they can trust us and many times they have protected us from more violent people on the streets. Finally, because of our relationship with the municipal government approximately 38 people that we referred to a government housing program received housing.

Churches and volunteers

The churches that have been involved with the project have been awakened to the needs around them and have developed a more holistic theology. Many volunteers have been converted during their time with us and some have decided to become missionaries. The volunteers receive periodic training and theological teaching through the project, resulting in their own increased theological reflection. We have received interns from the Evangelical Center of Missions, who come for training in urban ministry and community missions. The churches and volunteers have been challenged individually and collectively to live a simple lifestyle and to take coherent steps toward a life that reflects the kingdom values of justice, joy and peace.

Municipal staff

Perhaps the most exciting impact was the spiritual conversion of the director of the municipal institution that collaborated with us in the city shelter. It was a very special moment for the whole team as we harvested fruit in a place where we had never intentionally planted.

Another exciting impact of our work with the municipality was the influence the project began to have on several municipal staff. Upon seeing our work, one policewoman began to give some of her time to cut the hair of poor women at the shelter. A policeman who had been well-known for mistreating street people came to the shelter one evening and encouraged the guests to lead a good life and listen to the staff at the center.

THE FUTURE OF THE REDEEMER PROJECT

To better minister to people's needs, we are convinced of the need to improve our training and recruiting program. We are also looking for part-time volunteers to lead the ministry and make new contacts. Two new projects that we hope to initiate in the future are helping mentally ill women and terminal HIV/AIDS patients, but funding for these projects is currently unavailable. We have begun talking about having our own rehabilitation and recovery home at the beginning of 1997, if the Lord permits. We have received a recent offer of an area of 48,000 square meters of land; this is still in the negotiation phase.

4

New life for the children, Brazil

Denise da Silva Maranhão

In the semirural, backwater town of Sabinópolis in the central Brazilian state of Minas Gerais, *Bem Estar do Menor* (BEM—Child Well-being) ministers to children and adults through child care centers and educational, agricultural and health programs. Since 1973 the sponsoring church, the Evangelical Missionary Pentecostal Church (IEMP—*Igreja Evangélica Missionária Pentecostal*), has grown from five to eleven congregations and from 200 adult members to over 2,000 members.

IEMP was founded in 1967 by Nicolaas and Trijnie van Eijk, a missionary couple from the Netherlands. Soon after their arrival in Sabinópolis they discovered that simply preaching the Word of God was insufficient. They began to assist new believers to escape poverty so that they could provide adequately for their families and no longer feel pressured to move to Brazil's large cities.

Since it was the children who suffered most, IEMP began a ministry oriented toward the needs of children. This ministry—BEM—has since expanded to include a variety of programs that serve the needs of whole families. BEM currently ministers directly to approximately 5,500 people and has 150 employees.

THE CONTEXT

BEM ministers in a rural region where the main economic activity

40

is subsistence agriculture. Since even the landowners can barely make a living, the landless must rely on other employment, such as sharecropping and other forms of farming. The rural areas are very poor and do not have the kind of infrastructure that encourages permanent settlement in the area. Many leave for the cities and resettle in the poor, marginal neighborhoods on the periphery of those cities. There they find dismal conditions often characterized by poor housing, unemployment and underemployment, low educational levels, alcoholism, family disintegration, incest and prostitution.

The region around Sabinópolis is very Roman Catholic. The people's traditional religion revolves around the patron saints (a practice considered by many to be idolatry), under a powerful orientation provided by the Roman Catholic church. There is little knowledge of Jesus or of the Bible.

The ministry works with low income families, particularly the peasants who live in the rural areas and those that have moved from the rural areas to the towns in the Sabinópolis area.

Causes of poverty in the area

- ❖ Uneven distribution of the land and income (in part caused by a law that gave squatters the right to own land after living and working on it for five years; the large landowners responded by removing the squatters from the land).
- ❖ Low educational levels.
- ❖ Low salaries.
- ❖ Alcoholism.
- ❖ Children abandoned during the day by mothers who need to work outside the home.
- ❖ Lack of knowledge of Jesus and the Bible.
- ❖ Idolatry.
- ❖ Lack of good teaching by the traditional church.
- ❖ Spiritual questions without answers.
- ❖ Poor public administration and lack of public policy to help the poor.
- ❖ Exclusion of many people from the social rights needed to promote human development.

41

When the BEM project began in 1967, the situation was as follows:

* There was a high level of malnutrition;
* The area had a public administration without the capacity or interest to intervene in social problems; and
* The city was controlled by a *caudillo* (an authoritarian leader who singlehandedly makes all the important decisions), whose power base was the local hospital.

Despite society's division and disintegration, the traditional church remains silent. The only discourse concerns the need to define the dogmas of the Roman Catholic Church, with no demonstration of an interest in the people or even in the church members. There was a Catholic leader who tried to initiate some social programs involving a school and a hospital, but to do so successfully he would have had to ally himself with the *caudillo*, who was both a physician and a political leader.

The people do not know who Jesus is; Mary is the central figure in their religious life. There was much persecution and hostility toward the early IEMP converts. Their dead could not be buried in the local cemetery. The van Eijks said that "initially we did not have any resources, just our house and the food we ate. The support for this project came from the members of our church [in Holland], who began to take part in helping the people. We knew nothing about social projects, we only knew about Jesus and his love. Later, the first converts also began helping the ministry."

DESCRIPTION OF THE MINISTRY

The first stage of the work began when the van Eijks shared their home, food and resources with needy people who requested help. After acquiring a house in Sabinópolis, they established a child care center for 40 children. The van Eijks had no technical knowledge of running such projects. They simply cared for the children as if they were their own, dealing with the most urgent needs—hunger, malnutrition or abandonment.

In 1973, a few years after the church had been started, the van Eijks and several other believers from the church who worked in the project founded BEM. This made it possible to enlarge the program to include food and clothing distribution, and housing construction. Over time several Christian professionals joined the BEM work team—social workers, an architect, a medical doctor, a teacher and a psychologist—allowing us to expand and systematize the work.

In 1980 we established educational community centers (ECCs) to attend to the needs of church and community members in their own neighborhoods and in rural areas where IEMP congregations had been established. We developed various projects with the local people based on their real needs.

The ECCs see their role as that of organizing and supporting community groups that are formed around specific needs. They motivate and raise awareness within the groups, training the participants to search for collective, self-help solutions to their problems. These problems have to do with neighborhood improvement, family or social education, worker training, health problems or student work. The principle that governs our efforts is to work with the whole family. We try to create the means by which parents can assume responsibility for their children. To accomplish this we use different methods: home visits, group meetings, interviews and food production activities (e.g., goats, community gardens, community stores, distribution of basic food products).

Currently the ECCs are involved in the following:

1. *Student support program*: Involves school snacks and meals, sports and leisure activities, evangelization and instruction regarding life in general. There is also work with the children's families. Two hundred children are involved.

2. *Mothers' groups*: Involves educational meetings covering areas such as health, family relationships, evangelization, environment, self-esteem, manual arts and production. Sixty mothers are involved.

3. *Youth groups*: Involves educational meetings on subjects such as health, sexuality, education, evangelization, professionalism, sports, manual arts, personal and family orientation. There are 80 teenagers involved.

4. *Family gardens*: For production of vegetables to improve the families' diets and for sale. Seventy-two families are involved.
5. *Community plots*: For growing coffee, millet, yucca, beans, bananas, squash. Thirty families work with these.
6. *Raising goats*: Fifteen families are involved in this project to improve their diets.
7. *Other projects*: Work with 40 high school students, a youth center for 80 youth, and two rural schools teaching grades 1-4 to 70 students, adult education, Bible teaching (in all programs), food production for use in BEM programs and systematic training of BEM workers.

Through a systematic training program the new converts eventually assumed leadership of the project. Today, there is a new generation of young people and families that were formed in the church and involved in the work. They are the leaders of the social projects. They received help in the past and now they are helping others. People who were excluded in the past today have access to schools and other basic services. Despite the preconceptions to the contrary, this provides a testimony that believers are different in their daily lives.

Most of the financial support has come from foreign sources such as child sponsorship through the mission from the Netherlands and funds from TEAR Fund, Belgium, and TEAR Fund, Holland. Another 30 percent comes from local sources such as BEM's production activities, local donors and the state government.

WHAT ARE THE RESULTS?

With the new alternatives, families have a healthier diet because of their gardens and goat raising. Malnutrition among children served by the child care centers is now maintained at less than 3 percent. In 1995 the index used to measure long-term malnutrition was lowered by 6 percent. In 1995 the animal husbandry program involved 384 goats, 992 hens, 71 head of cattle, 15 beehives and a few geese—all contributing to the nutrition of the children in the child care centers or the families themselves. The community gardens—involving about 400 people—yielded over 5,000 kilograms of produce. This is in addition to the fruit and vegetables BEM produced for use directly in its own programs or for sale, as well as produce measured other than by weight.

The heightened awareness of the importance of education has resulted in the people achieving a higher level of education. It used to be a struggle to finish the fourth grade; now, many make it through the second year of high school. Of the 335 students in BEM's child care centers, 299 (89.3 percent) passed in 1995.

The families are more responsible with their children—not just in the economic aspect, but also with general upbringing and discipline. They are more conscious of their rights. They are more involved in society in general. They have organized themselves and have participated in the election of local public officials. They have a better concept of what it means to be citizens.

The values of the people have changed. They emphasize the priority of the family. The families have also seen an improvement in their economic level. Most own their homes and keep them in good condition.

The most noticeable spiritual changes are seen in the ways in which people deal with their day-to-day problems and their relationships with family members, neighbors and society in general. There is still a lot of criticism and pressure from some Catholics, however, because many families have left the Roman Catholic Church.

Six new churches have been planted since 1973 (three since 1980). Adult membership has grown from 200 to over 2,000. Most of this growth occurred since 1980, when the education community centers opened.

How People Have Come to Know Christ

People have come to know Christ as much through project meetings as through the churches. Many came to know Jesus through their parents, neighbors or through a local mothers' group, youth group or children's project. Other people work in the mission, listening and seeing the difference in the lives of their colleagues.

Many came to know Christ through the healing of their physical ailments. The Christian community gave them a new perspective on life—one with more meaning and with hope for the future. There is always a biblical basis for whatever topic is discussed in the groups. The children and adolescents receive Christian teaching daily in the projects.

Through the systematic training of the project workers, we try to renew the vision that we are a "mission" and that one of our responsibilities is to transmit the Good News. The leaders of the projects are also leaders in the churches; in this way the two areas complement each other. We have seen people come to know the Lord Jesus Christ through the activities of the projects and the churches.

The social projects are directed toward fellow believers and to all interested people in the communities where the projects are operating. The Christians participate in the growth of the community with a different perspective regarding community behavior and organization, and pursue objectives that benefit the whole community.

EVALUATING THE PROJECT

Factors that contributed to the project's success:

❖ Responding to the changing reality of the people and their needs;

❖ Emphasizing the project's goals, objectives and philosophy to all project workers; and

❖ Seeking partners that are willing to invest time and money with us.

Obstacles to the project's success:

❖ A lack of skilled people who share a vision for a more holistic approach to mission;

❖ The lack of a greater number of capable church leaders; and

❖ The traditional church has discouraged people from participating in BEM's programs out of fear that they would convert to a different church. Also, the genuineness of the faith of new believers is often questioned because they have received help from BEM.

Some things that could have been done differently to improve the work would have been to establish better relationships with the local and state governments and to have worked more with small farmers. The state government has given some financial support to BEM but the local government has been less helpful and even been a hindrance to the ministry.

5

Conserving the soil and cultivating the church, Nicaragua

Uriel Tercero

The Assemblies of God churches in the northern region of Nicaragua have begun helping their members and their neighbors through a soil conservation program. The leaders of these churches started this program in March 1993, which has promoted and taught the use of contour ditches, live barriers, green manure, windbreaks, reforestation, natural pesticides, nontraditional crops and family gardens.

Members and nonmembers of Assembly of God churches have participated in this program. Because of the church's improved image among the unchurched, along with the testimony in word and deed of the program promoters and other church members, the congregations have experienced an average growth of 36 percent between 1994 and 1995.

This growth rate is three times the average annual growth of 11 percent between 1984 and 1994. The total membership of these congregations has risen from 2,046 adults to approximately 2,781 adults from 1994 to 1995. Two congregations have doubled their membership during this one-year period.

The growth of the churches has influenced the social life of the communities. In one case, the two *cantinas* (bars) of a community were closed down because their owners became Christians. Local philanthropy has been promoted through tithes of agricultural products to local charities.

THE CONTEXT

Northwestern Nicaragua (the departments or provinces of Estelí, Madriz and Nueva Segovia) is mainly rural and has a variety of climates—arid, semiarid, and a few semihumid areas.

During the war between the Contras and the Sandinistas in the 1980s, this area suffered much armed conflict. This caused many people either to migrate to other Nicaraguan towns or to Honduras, or to join the fighting with one of the several irregular fighting forces. During this period the people abandoned the coffee, livestock and basic grain farms. This caused an economic crisis, and the lives of the area's inhabitants became extremely difficult.

This was the prevailing situation when the war ended shortly after the 1990 election of Violeta Barrios de Chamorro as president. This change brought about conditions that allow for employment, the satisfaction of social and economic needs, and for reconciliation among the peasant farmers (*campesinos*) and the general population because of the friction caused by political divisions and crisis.

At the time of the new government's triumph, there was a certain mistrust among the people toward organizations and institutions. The people feared that these powers may have intentions other than a desire to help, and that the people would become involved in political matters. This climate favored the work that the church could do, since the church did not take sides and had declared itself apolitical during the country's hardest times. This precedent enabled the church to have a good outreach today.

Much of the area's population was economically poor since they were short of money, food and work. Now the people are beginning to understand that their environment is full of valuable resources from which they can benefit. Social poverty exists, caused at least in part by the social disintegration due to the wars, and instability still

49

continues in some regions. The fruits of this disintegration are delin-
quency, drug abuse, kidnapings, robberies and deaths.

Many did not have Christ in their hearts, leading to lives of spiritual
and material poverty. There was no correct teaching of the gospel;
there was paganism or a religiousness without any true conversion.

The influence of Roman Catholicism has been significant and
almost official. The majority (at least 80 percent) of the population
belongs to the Roman Catholic Church, but there is a great degree
of nominalism. During the 1980s the evangelical churches experienced great growth. We estimate that the Assemblies of God
churches in the communities currently involved in the agricultural
program grew at an average rate of 11 percent between 1984 and
the end of 1994.

Origins of the IDSAD[1] Social Project

In March 1993 a group of community leaders and a group of
church leaders met together. We were informed about the launch of
an agricultural project. The objective of this project was to promote
community development in an integrated manner based on sustainable, organic agricultural and environmental preservation programs among both men and women.

Our first activities included workshops on:

❖ Construction, calibration, and use of the "A" frame agricul-
tural level
❖ Natural insecticides
❖ Soil fertility measurement

With time we have carried out other activities:

❖ Soil conservation (green manures and compost, contour
ditches, live barriers, windbreaks)
❖ Reforestation and living fences
❖ Cultivating plants for pesticide production
❖ Family gardens
❖ Cultivating food staples with improved techniques
❖ Nontraditional crops
❖ Providing cows to pastors through a revolving program

Some subjects discussed in subsequent workshops include: integrated development, biblical principles for development, soil conservation, green manures, the importance of vegetables, integrated control of plagues, managing family gardens, natural insecticides and compost.

We began with three agricultural promoters working in 23 communities. At the end of 1995 there were four promoters working in 31 communities with an overall participation of 870 people—536 men and 334 women.

The participants include active members of Assemblies of God churches, active members of other churches and people that were not active in any church. In many cases the pastor participates in the program and in one case the pastor is the coordinator of the group in his community. We have received limited financial support from TEAR Fund-United Kingdom, technical assistance from World Relief-Nicaragua (and financial and administrative support since March 1996), in-kind donations from other international institutions such as the World Food Program and Food for the Hungry, and cooperation with similar organizations at a local level.

Faith in Christ has been shared with the participants in different ways—integrated in the training sessions, through devotional times led by the promoters or group coordinators, and through the informal sharing of faith among participants. In addition, the promoters further a good witness for Christ by:

❖ Teaching wholesome manners to the participants
❖ Distributing Christian literature, when available
❖ Praying during meetings and at field projects
❖ Prohibiting the use of profanity and the practice of vice within the groups

SOCIAL AND SPIRITUAL RESULTS

The constant witness of the gospel of Christ to the group participants has encouraged many to come or make a recommitment to Christ.

The program has also facilitated the peasant farmers' development of a sustainable agriculture that allows for a rational use of human, material, economic and social resources. The impact on the environment has been positive, since the inputs we work with are organic and are used in a sustainable manner. The soil is improving and there is reforestation. By September 1996 program participants had constructed over 90 kilometers of soil erosion barriers of different types, nine community nurseries for producing seedlings for reforestation had been established and the 547 women involved in the project had planted 290 family gardens.

With improved techniques, maize yields have increased from approximately 1,300 kilograms per hectare to 2,900 kilograms per hectare. In 1996, 261 hectares of maize fields were planted with improved techniques, with the implied increase in production from these fields of approximately 400,000 kilograms of additional maize. Bean yields have also more than doubled and approximately 80 hectares of beans have been planted in 1996 with improved techniques. Alternate crops such as pineapple, cacao, plantain, soy, and sesame have also been introduced with some already in the production stage.

The program has also had a tremendous impact on the social life of some communities.

Santa Teresa

The pastor and the church have played important roles in the project. In the past the community thought that the only thing the church did was have worship services. But now the church promotes practical activities, such as the cultivation of basic grains and family gardens.

Those who benefit from the program have made a commitment to return 10 percent of the harvest, which the local committee uses to help the community preschool. On one occasion a blind man was helped so that he could go to a clinic to receive treatment from a specialist. The pastor's family has also received assistance. But the greatest benefit has been the help that those who are directly involved in the program have received—a level of assistance that had never before been experienced in these communities.

Neighboring communities have observed what is happening and

are asking for technical advice, which the participating communities have gladly given. This has helped to launch new programs among both men and women.

Other positive changes have been noted in Santa Teresa. There used to be two *cantinas* (bars) in this community, but today the owners have converted to Christ. Now there are no alcoholic beverages for sale in Santa Teresa, and no more fights associated with such sales. In 1995 the Assembly of God church has grown from 90 to 220 members, has experienced miracles and healings and has seen its members and adherents dedicated to greater faithfulness and obedience.

La Lima

Here one can clearly see the difference that these new agricultural practices have made, and the great interest that they have aroused among the people. This community has also helped its preschool with 10 percent of the vegetable harvest. Everyone—men, women and children—has come to realize the importance of sustainable agriculture and the use of garden produce for family consumption.

The cultivation of nontraditional crops such as pineapple, fertilizing beans (the velvet bean and jack bean), *quequisque* (a local root crop) and sugar cane is very noticeable in La Lima. The use of compost made from coffee hulls has also been popular, which has benefitted participants, since they no longer have to buy costly chemical inputs.

Condega

In this small town of about 10,000 people, the program has helped the *Comedor de Desarrollo Infantil* (Dining Room for Child Development), a center sponsored by the mayor's office where preschool children, children working on the streets and orphans come for meals. The project provides seeds, which some of the mothers plant on land provided by the center to produce some of the food for the children. We have also helped the center with some food provided by the World Food Program.

In each community the people want our help because they see that the project makes few promises, but there is much action and many positive results. Sometimes we have had to turn people down because of the high demand and the lack of resources and time to satisfy the needs of the communities. People in these communities are more aware of the importance of reforestation around rivers, other water sources and nonarable land, and the appropriate use of available resources.

How People Come to Know Christ

In our environment people accept Christ in a personal and individual way. But, soon after, their family members many times also make the choice to accept Jesus, and the work of God continues to grow.

Through the testimony in word and deed of the promoters and other church members, the congregations involved in the program have experienced an average growth of 36% between 1994 and 1995. This growth rate is three times the average annual growth rate of 11% between 1984 and 1994, and compares to an estimated 7.8% growth rate for all the evangelical churches in Nicaragua (Patrick Johnstone in *Operation World*, Grand Rapids: Zondervan, 1993).

We have already mentioned the tremendous growth in the church in Santa Teresa and the outstanding changes in this community. An important factor in this change is the image the church now has in the eyes of the community. Another factor is the direct participation of the pastor as coordinator of the group involved in the agricultural program. We must also acknowledge the work of the Holy Spirit in the community.

Condega, an urban center, has had a different experience. We have preaching groups in six areas of the rural communities and we have six such groups in the city. In these places we are developing leadership, improving the attention people receive and experiencing a growth in membership. For example, in December 1994 we had 119 members; on December 31, 1995, we had 223 baptized members and 40 membership candidates.

In the city we have meetings in private homes on Tuesdays and Thursdays, and in the church we have services on Wednesdays,

Saturdays and Sundays. There are also meetings with church leaders for prayer and planning. Participants from all the different groups meet together once a month for Holy Communion.

We also visit hospitals, the police and the homes of believers and nonbelievers in need. Members of the church participate in these activities. In addition, every member takes part in evangelization activities.

In the rural areas, selected lay workers help the community with social and spiritual matters. In the social area we support work that the local government is promoting, such as building schools, latrines, roads and health centers.

The local church in Condega plans to establish two new congregations (besides the three congregations it has already founded and that are now autonomous). The church in Condega also helps support missions by giving 10 percent of its tithes to help those who found new churches. The churches in other communities have also experienced growth; the most important factor in this growth was the church's testimony in deeds and words.

We can find an example of this in the area of Quilalí, some 200 kilometers north of Condega. Ten churches participate in the soil conservation and family gardens programs. The participation and support of the pastors has been vital to the success of the work and to carrying out the project's material and spiritual tasks. Now churches are seen as valuable and worthy of respect, honor and recognition.

In the area of Somoto, some 30 kilometers west of Condega, the results vary. In the places where the pastor is involved, the results of the work and the participation of the people have been very good. When enthusiastic and active lay people are involved, there is great progress and success in the work.

EVALUATION

Outside observers have commented very positively on the process and results of our experiences with development and the church. We hope to do even more in the future. However, sometimes the obstacles are more apparent than anything else:

- ❖ The country's sociopolitical problems
- ❖ The lack of financial resources
- ❖ The need for an office in the work area
- ❖ The lack of a comprehensive and timely accounting system in the central offices for handling funds from abroad
- ❖ The lack of vehicles for mobility to facilitate the work
- ❖ Some communities are almost impossible to reach with a vehicle
- ❖ The lack of appropriate and sufficient training materials
- ❖ The inability to respond to all of the communities who would like to organize themselves and the lack of resources to support them in their efforts
- ❖ The lack of active support by some pastors
- ❖ In the Somoto area, the people's mentality of only receiving handouts, caused by a history of emergency relief

We have confronted these and other obstacles with creativity and dedication, sometimes to the point that the promoters have paid for their transportation and have bought workshop materials out of their own pockets. Since March 1996, World Relief's direct participation and support has helped us overcome many of the obstacles mentioned above.

Finally, one thing that we would do differently is a better job of raising the awareness of the pastors so we could have their full support for our work in their communities.

NOTE

1 *Instituto de Desarrollo Social de las Asambleas de Dios* (Social Development Institute of the Assemblies of God) or IDSAD. IDSAD has been renamed PRODAD (*Programa de Desarrollo de las Asambleas de Dios*—Development Program of the Assemblies of God).

6

The Office for Social Advancement and Development, Colombia

Rosa Camargo

The Office for Social Advancement and Development (OPDS—*Oficina de Promoción y Desarrollo Social*) was founded in April 1990. It came about in response to the demands of a holistic gospel which orients individuals, groups and communities toward spiritual, economic and social development.

THE CONTEXT

Microenterprises

From the beginning OPDS focused on the needs of small business people in smaller scale enterprises who, because of their marginal condition, had no access to formal bank credit. Most of these small business people are women (70 percent) who work in activities such as dressmaking, breadmaking, food production and sales, the production and sale of handicrafts and the sale of miscellaneous products. Many of them are heads of families as single, abandoned or widowed mothers. The remaining 30 percent are men engaged in small-scale commercialization of food or clothing, the making and selling of shoes and furniture or owning and operating small appliance repair or vehicle repair shops.

Most of the microenterprises are at a cottage-industry level. The shoemaking and furniture shops include both modern and obsolete tools. Food production is done without chemical preservatives and so the products are highly perishable.

Those involved in retail sales range from street vendors to small business people with permanent and relatively well organized business locations. Service businesses include barber shops and restaurants, in addition to the repair shops already mentioned.

The microenterprises that the program focuses on are primarily one-person or family businesses. The businesses that have employees have no more than five. Each business has working capital of no more than US$5,000. Monthly sales range from US$500 to US$3,000.

The region

There are inherent factors in the nation's development that explain why, after Chocó, the north coast is the poorest region in Colombia. Two of the factors are the exaggerated centralization of government administration and the violence that has dislocated large numbers of people from the countryside to the cities in recent years. These people, who are accustomed to an agrarian culture, move to cities like Barranquilla and Cartagena without knowing how to earn a living and without prospects for finding formal employment. The more fortunate begin as helpers in small shops where they learn a trade and aspire to own a shop eventually.

The poor of the north Colombian coast are poor not only because they lack economic resources but also because they have lost their cultural heritage by leaving the countryside for the city. They have lost their friends and, what is even sadder, they have lost their self-esteem and self-respect. In the marginal areas of the cities we can often see how families disintegrate for these reasons, more than for the lack of money.

The program

The development of the microenterprise program followed the biblical model of starting at home, extending to the surrounding community and continuing to widen its reach. For this reason evangelical believers were the first to benefit from the program. They were followed by their non-Christian friends and finally by the community in general. Presently 54 percent of program participants are Catholics or non-Christians, and the remaining 46 percent are evangelical Christians from different denominations (Presbyterian, Baptist, Assemblies of God, Pentecostal).

The program has a valuable resource in the members of the OPDS board of directors, who are Christian professionals with a high commitment to the work of God and a clear vision of holistic development through the church and the church's commitment to the community. Equally important for the program's success and development has been the participation of the local church in each of the seven Colombian cities where the program is operating. The local church contributes volunteer workers and space for an office. The microentrepreneurs contribute their enthusiasm and do the work of promoting the program among their friends, neighbors and acquaintances.

PROGRAM DESCRIPTION

The microenterprise program provides microentrepreneurs with credit, training and counsel. The associated methodologies of solidarity groups and communal banks were selected for the program's credit management, which has been a contributing factor to the program's success. These methodologies have permitted the healthy mixing of Christians and non-Christians, experienced business people with novices and buyers with sellers, giving an interesting dynamic of holistic development to the group. No loans are given to those involved with the sale of cigarettes, liquor or illegal substances.

When groups of believers who wish to join the program are formed, they are given training and then encouraged to share the information with their friends. They bring their non-Christian friends into the program who, in turn, bring their friends, too. But because believers are the vehicles for bringing about entry into the program, they are in a privileged position to share their faith. People who have never wanted to hear about the gospel open their ears to what these Christians—who are willing to share their economic blessings—have to say.

After they participate in the program, we have learned that people who never wanted to accept an invitation to go to church no longer had this attitude because they had lost their wariness toward evangelicals. By participating in the program, they had developed bonds with church people so that they no longer felt like strangers when they visited a church.

The microenterprise program also provides training in administrative and accounting subjects. These training sessions are held in churches. This further helps lessen any apprehensions about going to a Protestant church.

Personalized counsel is given to each micro business person. This builds bonds between the adviser and the micro business person and also helps create opportunities to share Christian values and faith.

But the most effective contribution that the microenterprise program has made to the evangelization work of the local churches is that microentrepreneurs have become witnesses to God's love and power. It is amazing to see how people who for years have had a low profile in the church have blossomed. With the opportunity to invite their friends into the program, their self-esteem has grown and they have become leaders within their groups and their community as well as effective evangelists. Some take their old and new friends to the church to hear the word. Others teach directly, but the important thing is that the church is multiplying the number of believers who share the gospel with others.

The microenterprise program has also brought economic development to the churches since their income has increased through tithing and the increase in membership. Churches of different denominations are involved in each of the seven cities where the program operates.

RESULTS

The results of the program have been amazing and we are convinced that the power of God has supported our work all these years. The program has assisted a little over 2,000 families whose income basically depends on microenterprise activity. With increased income these families have improved their nutrition, their children's education and their living conditions. Most important, the self-esteem of participants has improved and their confidence that God is their true provider has been strengthened.

The local church has enhanced its position within the community because the community recognizes the work that is done. An example of this happened in El Carmen de Bolívar, where one of the Christian business persons was chosen town councilman—the first time that a Christian has occupied this post.

A highly gratifying aspect is the change that we have seen in the physical, emotional and spiritual aspects of women participating in the program, particularly those women who have been abandoned by their husbands or who are heads of households for other reasons. Generally when they enter the program they seem dispirited, but as their businesses prosper they begin to blossom, their appearance improves, their self-esteem grows and they look happy.

The churches too have benefitted from the development of these women as they develop into leaders with great potential. A typical example is Magdalena González in Cartagena, of the Christians in Action Church who, with five small children, was abandoned by her husband. When she joined the program she was as noticeable as a shadow, but after two years she has become a community and church leader. All her children are in school and her dressmaking business has experienced extraordinary growth.

HOW THE PEOPLE COME TO KNOW CHRIST

The microenterprise program directly involves at least one church in each city and indirectly all the churches that wish to participate. There are three ways that a church can participate in the program: 1) through providing leaders for the program committees; 2) through volunteers that cooperate in the development of the program; and 3) through microentrepreneurs.

As mentioned earlier, when the groups first form believers are given the opportunity to invite their non-Christian friends to participate. This provides an opportunity for these friends to come to church and creates bonds of friendship and fellowship that ultimately are the keys to their willingness to listen to and accept the gospel. We have the testimony of leaders in the seven cities where the program is currently operating that their churches have grown through the testimony that has been given by the microentrepreneurs.

The average attendance in these churches was 114 in 1990 and rose to 390 in 1996. This represents an average annual growth rate of about 23 percent. The pastors estimate that about 25 percent of the new members came into contact with their churches though the social ministry. Some churches grew more dramatically. An example is the church at Blas de Lezo, which grew to 750 people, and planted four additional congregations.

Another that grew quickly is a church in Medellín, which grew from 25 people in 1990 to 150 today. Two churches located in the very heart of the most violent area of the city implement the program there. The program has had tremendous impact in the community, because in these places the common practice is "kill to survive." But these churches are teaching in a practical way that one can love and share to survive. There are 62 families in the program, most of whom were not believers but who are now learning not only how to earn a living by legitimate means, but also an entire philosophy of nonaggression and mutual help.

FACTORS THAT HAVE CONTRIBUTED TO THE GROWTH OF THE CHURCH

1. Generally speaking the people who actively work in evangelism and discipleship in our churches are those with so-called "spiritual" gifts, e.g., evangelists, musicians, pastors. The gifts of administration and service are infrequently trusted or used, because they are not considered "spiritual." Some churches do not even know that these gifts form a part of the body of Christ. The micro business project has given opportunities to professionals who felt frustrated because they could not use their talents in the church. Now they can do so. It has also recovered for the church the potential of

many microentrepreneurs who felt marginalized and even under-esteemed.

2. The mindset of church leaders has changed. This was perhaps the critical part of the project, because we could not have developed it if the leaders had not eventually accepted the idea that service is part of the Christian life and that it can be a basic factor in the church's development. This process continues today, and the Holy Spirit has been essential to this since it is the Spirit who has raised up a new generation of leaders with a renewed vision of the holistic work of the church.

3. The community has stopped seeing the church as a religion or just another sect, but has begun to see it as a community of people who live out and share the love of God.

The role of the project personnel

The project staff have carried out the task of discovering potential leaders with administrative or service gifts and of inviting them to become part of the project. They have also guided microentrepreneurs to the opportunity they have to be witnesses of God's love to their friends and neighbors. Each church has been given the freedom to develop its own plan of evangelism. Churches in some cities have emphasized a person-to-person approach. Others use training meetings to share the gospel, and still others make door-to-door visits to each micro business person.

In its initial phase, OPDS shared its vision of integral or holistic work for the extension of the gospel with the leadership of the churches. In many ways this was a new concept for many of them and it naturally generated several reactions. This process lasted for about three years until there was sufficient understanding and acceptance to begin the direct work with the churches.

EVALUATION

Fundamental factors for the success of the project include:

1. *The recognition that without the direct participation of the local church we would not achieve the project's goals* in terms of evan-

gelization and the qualitative growth of the church. When projects for social and economic assistance are initiated it is always a temptation to develop them independently of, or parallel to, the church, because it is much easier to work exclusively with qualified personnel. The path we chose takes more time but produces better results.

2. *The recognition that the support of the church leadership is essential.* If the leaders are not convinced of the need to support the project it is better not to do it. Our project failed in one city where the leaders were not committed to it. It never grew at the expected rate and we finally had to terminate it.

3. *The recognition that we need to be trained for the task that we have been given.* We should be ready to pay the price in terms of time and money to become experts in the area of microenterprise.

4. *The recognition that God is the Lord of our work* and that the vision God has given us will be realized in God's time, not in ours. I received the vision for this work in 1985, but only in 1990 was it possible to begin the project. In 1986 I tried to start something but it ended in failure. It was then that I understood that if I wanted to serve in the work of God I would have to learn to wait for God's time.

7

Women in transformation, Colombia

Débora de Arco

The Christian Social Project of World Vision Colombia is located in the poor, marginal *barrio* (neighborhood) of Aguablanca on the outskirts of the city of Cali, Colombia. The inhabitants of Aguablanca suffer from hunger, unemployment, illiteracy, discrimination and a lack of educational opportunities. Unjust power structures impede the poor's access to development.

The women of Aguablanca tend to be the worst off in the community. They are also victims of domestic violence, a product of the *machismo* that permeates the culture. This violence is both physical and psychological and can be exacerbated by a literal imprisonment in their own homes without access to extended family, work and educational opportunities, or leisure activities. Besides all this, many women in Aguablanca are sexually abused. Forced to remain at home, these women must live in solitude, cut off from society and all meaningful discourse with other people.

In addition to the daily domestic realities that women face in Aguablanca, the *barrio* lacks most public services such as clean water, sanitation and sewage. Most of the houses are built of impermanent materials on eroding hillsides. Women are often the ones who must feed and take care of their families in the face of this reality. Spiritually, many of the inhabitants have only a vague knowledge of God. They believe that God is distant and absent from the problems that they face day in and day out. Others believe that God is a harsh authoritarian interested only in punishing those that do wrong. Finally, some do not believe in God's existence.

WORLD VISION'S WORK IN AGUABLANCA

In response to the needs of these women, World Vision began to work with the mothers of children supported through the child sponsorship program. They started by gaining the confidence of the women and developing work groups. Eventually, these activities began to respond to the needs expressed by the women themselves. The project has been guided from the beginning by Christian principles, and several committed Christian women serve as promoters. For many promoters, this project has given them the opportunity to present an incarnational witness of the love of Jesus Christ for the poor in their midst.

The goal of the project is to transform the relationships between men and women in Aguablanca to bring about more equality for the women. This is accomplished through education and the legitimization of the role of women in the family, the community and society. The project seeks to help broaden the participation of women in the social, political, economic and ecclesiastical activities of the community. Finally, the project seeks to point women toward Christ as their ultimate liberator.

Project activities center primarily on women's groups that seek to uncover areas of need and promote self-esteem. These empowerment sessions have been successful in allowing women to dream new dreams and build their personal identities. They have also helped women to encourage one another to dialog with their husbands and seek ways to bridge their differences. Each group meeting begins with Bible study and prayer.

THE PROJECT'S IMPACT

There are currently nine functioning groups involving about 150 women in Aguablanca. After two years, they have achieved significant spiritual and material goals. The women who participated in the initial training groups support the activities of other women in different sectors of the community. The project has had an impact in the following areas:

Self-esteem

Various training sessions and workshops were conducted over the last two years. As a result of these workshops many women have expressed that their self-esteem has improved, they have learned to love themselves, they dress better, speak better, and take time for recreation, reading and chatting with friends. They have learned to be less timid in large group settings and to express themselves more openly.

Spiritual life

Many women have declared that their lives have changed spiritually as a result of the project. They feel God's presence in their lives, they read the Bible, pray and attend church more often. Most important, many have testified to the impact that this has had on their families, especially in the way they treat their children. Some speak of the positive change that this has had on their husbands. The community also views the gospel more favorably after seeing its impact on the lives of the women.

Family life

As a result of the training sessions for married couples, many women report that their husbands are changing in a positive sense and that their family relations are improving.

Social and communal life

As a result of the training session, approximately 300 women leaders are now working in Aguablanca to improve living conditions. They assist with organizing people to improve housing, build schools, start infant feeding centers and create small businesses. Ten of these women currently occupy important positions of leadership in cooperatives and grassroots organizations.

Education

Encouraged by the project, thirty women returned to school and are currently finishing their final year of secondary school.

Political life

The nine women's groups recently organized the first municipal women's meeting in Aguablanca. As a result, these women have now been granted access to several social programs run by the municipality. In addition, the women used the meeting to launch a national women's network to promote their activities and help other women benefit from their project. One of the women, Deysi Caicedo, was nominated by the women's groups to represent them in Beijing at the United Nations Fourth World Conference on Women.

Economic life

There are currently three small businesses operated by women that are functioning in Aguablanca as a result of the project's training sessions. Each of these businesses provides significant income for the families involved.

CONCLUSION

I believe it is important to present expressions from the women themselves. The following comments were made by the women of the project. They express what the project has meant for them. They reflect the importance of a holistic approach to working with women in communities.

- ❖ "I have learned that God is very important in my life and that I am important to him and to myself. I have confidence in myself."
- ❖ "The program has helped us to organize as a group. It has trained us and we have learned how to improve our relationship with God, with ourselves and with others."
- ❖ "The program helped us to seek help from the government and from other entities."
- ❖ "The project does as our Lord Jesus did: He taught us to fish. He did not give us a fish."

* "World Vision teaches us to gain the confidence to make important decisions, not just at a personal level, but also at a community level."

* "We realized that we are a part of the community and that we have to work with ethics and morals, with faith and love for others."

* "I have learned that men and women have the same rights."

* "World Vision opened new possibilities of participation in the poor communities. We learned about Christian values in order to build better relations."

* "I am so happy with this group. I used to be an incurable gambler and I didn't take care of my home. I wasn't interested in caring for my husband or children. My husband always gave me money for food, but I would only buy rice and eggs for my children and use the rest on playing bingo. I would stay out late and I would get angry with my husband if he said anything to me about this."

* "As a result of the workshops I was able to reflect on my behavior and I decided to change my lifestyle. The most important thing is that I have the money that I used to spend on bingo. My husband is very happy and he encourages me to continue attending the women's group because our whole family benefits from it. In addition I am working with the mothers in the community and I am a leader in the group; I also work as a promoter in the solidarity network. I have gained credibility in my family, which used to mistrust me because of my lifestyle. Now the members of my family ask me for advice and I share with them the things I am learning. I thank God for the inclusion of women in the project and I encourage other women to participate in the different groups."

* "I want to share with you how my life has changed since I began participating in the women's group and the help committee of the project. My life was very depressing, so much so that I didn't want to talk with anybody. I also abused my eldest son, who was 11 years old at the time. Other people

would always yell at me, so I would wait for my husband to get home so I could berate him. Every day I was nagging and I sounded like a broken record. I didn't even greet my neighbors and when I did, I did so very aggressively."

❖ "My husband was always drinking due to my bad moods and we didn't respect each other. On many occasions we would end our arguments by beating each other. My marriage was going to end and I thought a separation would be best. I began working on my divorce. One day some people came to visit me and it was like seeing a light in a dark tunnel. I began to discover who God is. I began to understand that I should forgive my husband. I began to understand that you reap what you sow. I haven't changed everything, but I have begun a slow healing process in my life."

❖ "For me the change is very real. My children get the best grades at school. They are very understanding with their friends. They are not fighting about foolish things. My husband does not stay away as he did before. He is concerned about his children and about me. I became concerned about my personal appearance and without even noticing it I became known in my community as a leader in the neighborhood."

❖ "My family participates in several recreational activities. We celebrate special days with others from the group, like Christmas, Friendship Day, Women's Day. We have participated in wonderful workshops about how to understand men, avoiding gossip, accepting yourself as a woman and accepting others. I am very happy that I belong to the Christian Social Project and I am very grateful for the team that is doing this work. They are: Irma, Marina, Haudy, Martha, Olga Ins and Fabio. They are all very special. If I am a new person it has happened thanks to God and you."

8

Incarnating the gospel in Bolivia

Ivan Delgado

David Mamani is a committed believer who, as president of the community irrigation committee, labors diligently to ensure that the water needs of the community's farmers are met and the irrigation system is maintained adequately. Julián Ramirez is a dedicated Christian and community health worker who is actively involved in his church and in attending to the health needs of the members of his community. Fermín Toco shepherds the growing flock of believers at the evangelical community church and has also served successfully as community mayor.

These three people have several things in common. They are Christians who are part of a growing group of believers in Juntavi, Bolivia; they became Christians via the incarnational witness of a Food for the Hungry agricultural development promoter; and they all became intimately involved in helping to meet the physical needs of their neighbors as a result of their new-found faith. This combination is an exciting success story of both the impact of holistic ministry and the unfolding of Food for the Hungry's "Vision of Community" in Bolivia.

A VISION OF JUNTAVI

Juntavi is a small rural community of 300 inhabitants wedged into a deep, isolated canyon in the highland valley region of central

Bolivia, one of the poorest and most food-insecure areas in the country. The community is composed of members of two of the largest ethnic groups in Bolivia—the Quechua and Aymara.

Although located in the poorest region of Bolivia, Juntavi's physical infrastructure is very impressive. A potable water system pipes clean spring water to a tap in every household courtyard, an irrigation system allows community farmers to extend their growing season and increase production, a health network provides preventive education and basic curative services to all community members, greenhouses produce high-nutrient vegetables in several of the household courtyards and the primary school is adequately maintained.

In socioeconomic terms, the community is doing very well. Agricultural production not only meets average household consumption needs, but also provides income via the sale of surplus commodities. Potable water is abundant, with each community member receiving on average of 50 liters per day (166 percent of the amount recommended by UNICEF). Morbidity and mortality rates for women and children have dropped significantly and most of the women know how to treat diarrhea and respiratory infections, the major causes of childhood deaths.

But the community is not content to simply rest on its laurels—they want to make sure that progress continues. To that end, they have organized three committees to maintain and improve their services. The irrigation committee is in charge of maintaining and repairing the current infrastructure, and decides on the amount and timing of water distribution and adjudicating complaints. The health committee is in charge of overseeing the purchase and maintenance of medical supplies and the planning of maternal-child health courses for community women. Finally, the potable water committee is in charge of maintaining and repairing the water system.

In addition, information-sharing and informal training are occurring in various sectors of the community. The adoption of new agricultural technologies is occurring via direct farmer-to-farmer communication and training. New mothers are learning improved health care from experienced mothers. Committee and community members share knowledge about maintaining water and irrigation systems. All this points to a dynamic community development process with good potential for the future.

Spiritually, Juntavi has a growing group of Christians comprised of 40 committed members and several others who attend gatherings less frequently. These Christians meet several times a week for Bible study, worship and teaching in a building constructed with their own resources. They are also reaching out to neighboring communities with the gospel message.

That's exciting stuff. But probably the most exciting thing about Juntavi from a holistic viewpoint is the integration of the church in the daily life of the community. Julián, David, Fermín and other Christians exercise important roles in the development and oversight of the community. They do so out of their love for Christ and because of the example of the person who brought the gospel message to them. In return, the non-Christian community members respect and appreciate these Christians for their personal sacrifices in ensuring that people have water, good health and just government. That is the type of incarnation of the gospel that will continue to have an impact on Juntavi for years to come.

IT WAS NOT ALWAYS SO

The Juntavi of today is not the Juntavi of 1985, when Food for the Hungry began working there. At that time, it was a very poor, marginalized community. It had no road linking it to other major communities; agricultural productivity and production were very low, resulting in food insecurity; there was no potable water or adequate sanitation; childhood diseases and deaths were common; there were no health facilities and preventive health knowledge and practice were extremely limited. In addition, the prevailing belief system was a mixture of folk Catholicism and animism, resulting in a spiritual bondage that destroyed lives and undermined the material well-being of community members.

Juntavi was a poor Aymara community that had been marginalized by the predominantly Quechua neighboring communities, which were better off economically. Most of the households were engaged in subsistence farming and experienced food shortages during drought years. Local healers provided health care using traditional methods, which were often inadequate and linked to animism. The vast majority of the women in the community were illiterate.

In addition to material poverty, Juntavi suffered from spiritual poverty because of a worldview that mixed folk Catholicism and animism, resulting in the worship of the earth, the sun, the rain, the hills, the saints and the Virgin Mary. The result was not only a separation from God, but also a life of squandering what little resources the people had on drunken festivals, violent fights, sacrifices and food offerings to appease the gods, and traditional cures that produced little effect. An especially striking example of squandering scarce resources was the practice of sponsoring a festival. Each community member was required from time to time to "sponsor" a festival, which essentially meant providing all the food, alcohol and other necessities for a two-week binge. These festivals decimated the sponsor's entire household harvest of wheat and corn and most of his disposable income for one or even two years.

ENTER FOOD FOR THE HUNGRY

The reader probably now expects to read that Food for the Hungry entered the community and that made all the difference. But that is not the case, at least not in the beginning of the story. The truth is, nothing much changed during Food for the Hungry's first four years in the community. The organization was engaged in food-for-work programs and there was no permanent staff living in Juntavi. The results of that limited involvement were not very impressive. However, everything changed in 1989 with the arrival of a staff person named Paz Gutierrez, a dedicated Christian agronomist. Paz did several things that merit attention.

First, he lived in the community. He had daily contact with the people and began to interact with them about trivial as well as important things.

Second, he began with the spiritual by earnestly praying for change and sharing the gospel. His motto was: "If we win the community spiritually, then the material part will be added unto us." That was a pretty ambitious goal given that there was only one other evangelical Christian in the community when Paz arrived. But that was enough to start a weekly prayer and Bible study meeting in Paz's house. The two men prayed for a while and then invited a few others to attend. The astounding result was that at one point more than two-thirds of the community (200 people) came to those meetings, which had expanded into preaching and teaching sessions. Paz had a great gift as an evangelist and many responded to the message he gave.

Third, Paz worked hard to help community members develop economically and socially. He began to train interested farmers using simple but productive agricultural techniques. People planted vegetables for the first time and learned how to increase soil productivity and decrease erosion. Paz was not afraid of hard work and organized community work brigades to clean and repair the traditional irrigation system, which had fallen into disrepair.

Community members to this day comment that Paz worked harder than anyone else and always presented a good example of a biblical work ethic. He also reached out to the neediest people in the community by giving them used clothing and inviting them to share a meal with him. In all these activities, Paz took advantage of every opportunity to share his faith in Christ. Paz's sacrificial, incarnational living resulted in many community members coming to Christ, rejecting the bondage of the dominant worldview and beginning a life of outreach and service to their neighbors.

INCARNATING THE MESSAGE

After working in the community for a few years, Paz moved on to preach the gospel in other communities. Various projects and activities followed, including the construction of potable water and irrigation systems, an expansion of the agricultural training program, the establishment of a primary health care training program and discipleship classes for the newly-formed church. After Paz's departure, the number of believers in the church ebbed, but slowly began to grow again.

Eventually, Food for the Hungry pulled out of Juntavi in June 1995. Although the community members were sad to see the organization leave, they were confident in their ability to continue with the work. The seeds planted by Paz and others who followed after him had sprouted, taken root and were being nurtured by the community. The holistic witness of incarnational living had once again proven that God's message to the whole person is attractive and compelling, and many will respond when given the chance to see it lived out in their midst.

9

The cell group ministry in Peru

Atilio Quintanilla

Food for the Hungry International (FHI) in Peru is convinced that to have authentic development in needy communities, there must be an equal emphasis given to social and spiritual action, especially by churches. Social action that helps the poorest of the poor is a service of love born from the heart of God. When Christians engage in social action, it becomes a sacred act that is permeated by spiritual action. The Scriptures say, "Whatever you do, work at it with all your heart, as working for the Lord, not for men" (Colossians 3:23). Along these same lines, Tetsunao Yamamori wrote that "ministering to physical needs and ministering to spiritual needs, though functionally separate, are relationally inseparable, and both are essential to the total ministry of Christ's church" (see Appendix B).

THE CONTEXT

The communities where FHI is working are part of a poverty-stricken band of shantytowns that surround the city of Lima. Some of the inhabitants came to the shantytowns after fleeing terrorism. Others arrived as a result of the difficult economic conditions that made it impossible for them to afford good housing.

The needs in these communities are great. The people live on the sides of steep hills in houses made of bamboo mats without running water, sewage or garbage collection. They are materially poor and without stable work. Their incomes are very low, and most of them make a living as street vendors and day laborers.

The predominant religion in FHI work zones is Roman Catholicism. People generally attend church for baptisms, weddings and on special holidays. On these holidays they march in procession behind images of their patron saint, usually accompanied by a band. At night they have a party with the same band and drink until they are intoxicated. The evening often ends in fighting, with many men mistreating their wives and children.

A key cause of the poverty in these zones is the predominant culture of poverty, a result of years of being satisfied with just getting by without the people actively seeking to improve their situation. It has also been caused by the economic downturn that has plagued the country for the past 15 years, due in part to the terrorism practiced by the Maoist group, Shining Path, which forced many farmers to abandon their land and come to Lima for protection and better economic opportunities. After their arrival in Lima, the situation of many worsened because they had no land, no income and no homes. Families were forced to live on the sides of the hills in bamboo huts, with poor sanitation and little potable water.

Besides this physical poverty, the people's spiritual poverty comes from a lack of knowledge of the one true God and God's Word, and the fact that few have had an encounter with Christ. Their religious practices and customs include magic, spirit worship and idolatry through the worship of the land, the mountains, the sun and their ancestors. During the religious festivals, they march in procession to the crosses that are located on the hills, not as an act of faith but as an act of tradition.

Their social poverty and marginalization in this urban setting is due to the fact that many of these people have little formal education. They know how to cultivate fields and raise animals, but that knowledge serves them very little here. As a result, they toil as unskilled laborers, cleaners or street vendors, without many opportunities to improve their situation.

THE CELL GROUP MINISTRY PROGRAM

FHI began working through cell groups as a complement to its programs in health, microenterprise development and education. Cell groups are small prayer and support groups that meet in homes and ideally are connected to a larger church. Spiritual ministry through these cell groups accompanies and supports FHI's programs in diverse ways. A FHI team ministers to program beneficiaries through these groups, transmitting the message of salvation through devotionals, spiritual reflections, films, videos, visits and personal counsel.

In addition to providing support for FHI's programs, the cell group strategy focuses on working with Christian churches located in the project area. The first goal is to encourage these churches to develop a vision for holistic ministry. Later, the project team provides them with motivation, suggestions and training on strategies to strengthen and grow their congregations, enabling them to reach out to their communities and minister to the people in need.

The early church model

Both in theory and practice, we have learned that cell groups are a strong force for physical and spiritual development. In Acts 2:42-47, we see that the early church was one that met in small groups and sacrificially helped one another. The result was favor with the people, growth in numbers and satisfaction of needs. It would be difficult to expect the people in today's communities to sell their lands and homes to meet one another's needs, but the principle of the early church can still be applied. If Christians sacrificially share with one another, God's power and favor among people is released.

Our first cell group

The work with churches and cell groups was born out of the necessity to reach communities with the gospel. We realized that it was easier for the people to go to the home of someone they knew from their neighborhood than to go directly to a church. The willingness of Victoria Campos to offer her home for meetings motivated us to start a Bible study in 1994. The form of the meetings was changed little by little to meet the needs of those who were present. In the beginning, there were Bible study classes and prayer, combined with meetings of a social nature to celebrate birthdays, and talks for the young adults and for married couples.

The first group started with five people and soon began to grow. Victoria Campos asked for a helping hand from the Christian and Missionary Alliance Church of Rimac, which responded by sending two leaders and two teachers to support the cell group. As a result, 110 people attended the 1995 Christmas party. The average attendance at the time was 52 people, including children and adults. In March 1996 the group held a vacation Bible school for 110 children. The children enjoyed it very much and shared what they learned with their parents and families.

THE IMPACT OF THE CELL GROUP MINISTRY

Ministering to physical needs

God's love can be seen among the members of the cell groups as they combine what little resources they have to help other members in need. Twice they pitched in to help buy medicine for a little girl, Fiorella Calisaya, who had a very high fever. The doctors prescribed expensive antibiotics and her parents, who where poor, could not pay for them. They went to the hospital to feed her and pray for her. The cell group could not cover all of the expenses for the medicine, but the members prayed and God miraculously moved the hearts of the owners of a pharmaceutical laboratory, who decided to donate the needed medicine. Thanks to God, Fiorella was healed. The group members also helped a girl that came to the meetings barefoot. They combined their money to buy the girl a pair of shoes, and collected used clothing for children and teenagers who didn't have anything warm to wear in the winter.

A single mother and her one-year-old son stayed in the home of Victoria Campos, and for four months Victoria helped provide them with food while the mother was out of work. On another occasion the group collected money to give to Guillermo Saldana, who was suffering from neck injuries due to a car accident. The group also found a collar that they gave to Guillermo. These acts, though small, have ministered greatly to Guillermo, and were instrumental in bringing several of his family members to the cell group.

Finally, three-month-old twins Ronald and Steve Castro had to be hospitalized for heart and kidney problems. Upon hearing of this, several members of the cell group who met in the Castro family's neighborhood collected money and gave it to the Castros. They also prayed fervently for the twins' healing. When the boys were checked by the doctors, the heart problem had disappeared and the kidney ailment was improving. We believe that God worked this miracle, and the faith of the members of the cell group was strengthened greatly through it.

The church gets involved

Vishal Mangalwadi, in an address to FHI staff, said, "If God were to create a PVO [private voluntary organization], it would be the church. We believe that if churches today would live out a lifestyle as exhibited in the book of Acts, exciting and sustainable development would occur." The cell group ministry in Lima is convinced of this truth, and thankful that the first cell group's emphasis and growth soon caught the attention of other churches, especially the Palestine Pentecostal Church and the Peruvian Evangelical Church.

These churches invited our FHI team to help them form cell groups within their churches. We began training their leaders in how to lead a cell group. Through this experience, we came to understand the strategy of cell groups better, the opportunities they provide and the most effective methods to mobilize every church member to reach out to the community. Some members opened their homes for the meetings, others took on the roles of leaders and assistants, while others were involved in the work of discipleship, counseling and visitation. Because of the high level of motivation and commitment, we were able to train the church members in the development of this work, emphasizing the importance of expressing love in a practical manner, evangelizing through lifestyle and acts of compassion that others can see.

As a result, the Peruvian Evangelical Church formed 14 cell groups and the Palestine Pentecostal Church was divided into 15 groups. Six groups from each church are meeting regularly and enthusiastically. The others are still in the process of being formed, with the goal that the believers will catch the vision.

The major emphasis in the cell groups has been on the cultivation of Christian communion and friendship based on listening to each person's needs, analyzing problems together and encountering biblical solutions and practices. As a result, entire families have been strengthened, and group members pray for each others' work and health. Marriages in conflict have been reconciled. Participants have also been motivated to love others, help the church and take a class in basic Bible doctrine. The economic situations of at least two families have improved dramatically. The fathers have stopped drinking and can now invest money in the improvement of their homes and the education of their children.

The cell groups are expanding and more people are coming to know Christ. The Christian faith is shared in a natural way, with words as well as in acts of service and love. The people need to see and know the power of God at work, changing the lives of the people who believe in him.

Other results of the cell ministry

As a result of the work with the cell groups, the participants have become more sensitized to human needs. They have supported people in need in diverse ways. Fundraising activities, such as preparing and selling candy and food, have been used to help orphans and the sick. One such sale enabled the members to buy medicine, clothes and shoes for three orphans, who were brought to live in the community with their aunt. There have also been fundraising activities to help buy materials for the last vacation Bible school.

The nearby churches and their leaders have decided to adopt the cell-group strategy for their outreach ministries. There are groups that have grown to 35 participants, and many formerly passive church members are beginning to become more committed and involved. Finally, all of this has resulted in almost doubling the attendance at church meetings. The average attendance had been

50 to 55 members, and today an average of 100 people attend each church.

Other signs of meeting physical needs include cell-run first aid stations to offer medical attention to people who need it. Following the initiation of its cell groups, the Peruvian Evangelical Church held a "Health Day" several months ago. Five doctors volunteered to assist and saw 60 people that day. They charged a small symbolic fee for their consultation and gave out free medicine. This enabled the church to reach out to the community with very positive results.

The spiritual changes in the lives of people that are attending the cell groups can be seen in their testimonies. In some cases, alcoholics have stopped drinking. In other cases, violent people have changed their attitudes and behavior. Many have testified that the people who used to get into fights and hit their wives and children no longer do so.

Here are the statements of a few cell-group members:

* "It used to be that no one would come up to my hut to see me. They thought I was crazy and a troublemaker. You all have shown me the love of God." Julio Meneses

* "Praise God that my husband has lasted three weeks in a job and has stopped drinking! Before he would not even last a week because he drank too much and wouldn't finish his construction jobs." Gumercinda Meneses, Julio's wife

* "My uncle, Luis Alide, was very difficult and he would never think of kneeling to pray. He never wanted to come to my house because he told me that I never drink. Now, from morning to night the power of God is manifested in him, convinced through the testimony of my family. He, his wife, and his four children attend the cell group and participate in the games at our social gatherings." Antolin Huallpa, leader of a cell group of the Peruvian Evangelical Church

Members have begun to practice solidarity with their neighbors who are suffering or have problems. The people that attend the cell groups now participate more in the community assemblies, where before they would often criticize and mistrust the community leaders. As a result, several community leaders have also begun to attend the cell groups.

In addition, newly emerging Christian leaders have grown and been strengthened. In one cell group, two mature Christians who had not been involved in any leadership roles are now helping to lead the cell group and take responsibility when outside leaders cannot make it to meetings. Finally, the community is beginning to appreciate the cell groups as a forum for those who are seeking after God and where they can bring their needs before God.

Evaluating the Cell Group Ministry

There are several lessons we have learned that should help us in the future. One important principle is to limit the size of a cell group to a maximum of eight people, to maintain a high level of personal contact and discipleship. A new group should be started when the group grows beyond eight people. In addition, upon entering a new zone the ministry will attempt to identify the Christians in the communities and begin the work of starting the cell groups through them and their churches. We have seen that strong ties of friendship and fellowship, and helping out in practical ways are the keys to cell group growth, and we plan on strengthening these areas. Finally, leaders can be grown from within, and formal Bible training is not a prerequisite for leadership.

Conclusion

The latter part of Ephesians 5:25 states that Jesus gave his life for the church. We believe if Jesus were to take our place as a development practitioner, his strategies would result in a blessing to the local church. The combination of physical and spiritual ministry through cell groups captures some of the spontaneous power, favor and growth seen in the early church. We believe this cell group strategy is true to God's heart for reaching people in a holistic way.

Part two

Reflections

10

Latin American social contexts

Alva Couto

El pueblo gime de dolor (the people cry in pain), go the words of a Latin American song. That is the way most of our people feel, because they live in a very beautiful land, rich in natural beauty, but full of misery and violence. We know that much of the discussion in this book makes us feel pain, but we know also that we have hope, and we can search for alternatives. With that as background I would like to talk about holistic ministry that reaches people individually and in community, a holistic ministry for a devastated and divided context.

The song does not finish in pain; it continues beseeching God.

> Father, hear the cry of your people,
> Hear, Father, come and save us.

We have hope in Jesus, who gave his life to create a *new humanity*.

To talk about the Latin American context, we first have to talk about the model of society that was brought by the colonizers. We also must talk about other similar problems in the continent, the kind of society we live in today, and the ways we can have a holistic ministry in this society.

We want to understand the current situation and, in this reflection chapter, make a contribution to the evangelical church in Latin

America, so that it can participate in the social changes that our continent needs. "In the world, but not of the world, the church has a responsibility to the world, under its responsibility to God," a Brazilian writer has expressed it. As a church we have to work with alternatives of action that express even small signs of the kingdom of God, right where we are.

Finally, I will suggest some questions for our reflection, and themes for the agenda of everyone who participates in or manages holistic projects.

THE CONTEXT: BIG CONTINENT, BIG PROBLEMS

Often we read or hear about Latin America in the newspapers and on television. The information given to us does not always bring us joy. In this consultation, we asked the participants about the main problems in Central and South America. The subjects they mentioned and some of the aspects were:

In the political sphere:
❖ Formal democratization imposed by interests from abroad, and not through a process that arises from the people
❖ "Economization" of politics
❖ Corruption
❖ Attempts at integration
❖ Some good results in the fight for human rights

In the economic sphere:
❖ Passive acceptance of neoliberalism
❖ Growth of poverty and the concentration of wealth
❖ New forms of poverty
❖ Unemployment and underemployment
❖ Foreign debt that is unpayable, and countries continually going into debt
❖ The drug trade and its parallel activities

In the historical picture:
❖ Loss of values and no historical knowledge

In sociocultural areas:
❖ Violence

- ❖ Prejudice against women, single mothers, abandoned children
- ❖ Illiteracy
- ❖ Social-health system in bad condition
- ❖ "Homogenization" of the economy

In the religious area:
- ❖ Persistence of the Catholic-evangelical division
- ❖ Dominance of Catholic and evangelical conservatism
- ❖ Growth of neopentecostalism
- ❖ Growth of popular evangelical religiosity
- ❖ Growth of non-Christian religions

In the environmental sphere:
- ❖ Deforestation

In the area of local knowledge:
- ❖ Lack of information
- ❖ Communication system dominated by economic interests

Several researchers and social scientists from inside and outside Latin America have studied the causes of these problems in the economic, historical and cultural base. Among these social scientists, Celso Furtado (an economist) and Fernando Henrique (a sociologist), both Brazilians, developed the theory of dependence in the 1960s and 1970s. One of the main points of the Furtado research (1968) was to show how the evolution of international capitalism—with the fusion of powerful financial and industrial capital—at the end of the nineteenth and the beginning of the twentieth centuries influenced the Latin American continent.

In Latin American countries, the growth of large urban centers happened simultaneously with the growth of commercial activities, showing the specialization of countries in the areas of foreign trade and agricultural structures. The large income concentration created a new international division of production forces. Consequently, there was a large number of unemployed and underemployed workers who wanted jobs that the economic system could not create. These workers became a serious problem and a source of great social tension. In Brazil, especially in recent years, we have seen

89

how the international capital stream was one of the bases of economic concentration in multinational industries, of urban concentration (metropolization) and agricultural concentration (large landed estates and rural exodus). The state became a large presence in the economy.

Recent data from the UN report made by CEPAL (*Comisión Económica para América Latina y el Caribe*—Economic Commission for Latin America and the Caribbean) estimates Latin America's economic growth at 3 percent in 1996. In 1995 the growth was only 0.3 percent. Besides the insufficient growth, CEPAL points out signs of precariousness in work conditions and an increase of underemployment. The social backwardness and the huge inequality that characterize most of the countries of the region does not appear to have decreased over the years. The most optimistic side of the report is about the inflation numbers. In 1996, they were the lowest since 1972, but still they are high if we compare them to the international median.

Nowadays those who govern can decrease inflation and even end it, but they are unable to end corrupted politicians, businessmen and citizens. They are powerless to end the social problems and the misery that devastate millions every day.

This UN report, even while optimistic, does not hide the dichotomy between economic and social policy. There is a need to regain economic growth, but economic growth is necessary to improve basic social services—the social security system, the public health system, education, work and employment, and social work itself.

In brief, the usual situation in Latin America is instead of caring for society, opposing anarchy, supplying justice for all and ensuring the supply of goods and services, the state gives privileges to wealthy minorities and neglects the poor majorities. The modern state in Latin America has been an instrument of the dominant classes for their own gain and their own wealth, and they use the law to achieve their own objectives. There is a great divide between workers and the means of production. Misery becomes normal, and oppression is an instrument to keep order.

There is a need to return the state to its true role, that is to say, its role as a minister of God for the support of society and nature. Latin American society as it now stands is an iniquitous society that generates poverty.

HOLISTIC MINISTRY: TOWARD A CHANGE IN THE CONTEXT

In this continent, in this society, we are called to live and to respond to the reality of our time. But how are we to respond to that reality? How can Christians, representatives of the Latin American evangelical church, respond to this reality and keep their identity without compromising their faith?

Our answer is to have Jesus as a model. Jesus gives us the perfect model of service, and sends the church into the world with these words: "As [the Father] sent me into the world, I have sent [you] into the world (John 17:18)."

The manner in which Jesus served and conducted his mission in the world was dynamic: healing the sick, exorcising demons, praying alone, worshiping the Father and teaching us how to worship, reconciling people, bringing justice and peace, instructing the disciples. That is the complete, holistic way we must follow. Wadislau Martins Gomes, writing about the life of the church, says: "The Brazilian church, if it wants to be the church sent, must know its time and must change." We can apply this idea to the entire Latin American church. That is why we need to know our context well, and to act in the various Latin American realities in a dynamic way, looking to our model—Jesus Christ.

Holistic ministry demands vertical and horizontal relations. Our actions as Christians and as a church must be balanced between the vertical relation with God and God's Word and the horizontal relation with our neighbors and the world, as we can see in Figure 10.1 on page 92.

Instruction means to preach the gospel, to give advice, to comfort, to teach doctrine. As a part of evangelization people need to know what they believe in, and how and why they believe. But instruction by itself is not everything, because the gospel is not just knowledge. *Fellowship* with brothers and sisters in the faith is also

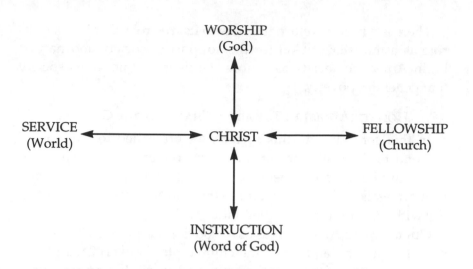

WORSHIP
(God)

SERVICE
(World)

CHRIST

FELLOWSHIP
(Church)

INSTRUCTION
(Word of God)

Figure 10.1. Balancing our vertical and horizontal relationships

necessary. God uses fellowship to improve instruction and transform it into love. Love is the fruit of our responsibility before God and before our neighbor. This love is so great that it makes us think about the greatness of God, our Creator and Savior. Then we can practice *worship* and adoration, our response to the grace of God. As we worship God we start to perform acts of *service* toward Christians and non-Christians.

These four important factors are essential to the life of the church and to Christians, particularly, to create a balance and to give a complete and holistic spiritual health to both. We can affirm that this is how vertical and horizontal relations must be in contemporary Christian thinking. Some theologians call it a theology of the holistic mission of the church.

Today there is a wider understanding of the meaning of this theology, but there are still some difficulties in completing a holistic practice of ministry. The way we think has been influenced by Greek Aristotelian philosophy that separates material and spiritual things, sacred and secular, man and woman. There are also historical reasons that influence the way we think, such as the First World missions that came to our continent. With all these influences, most evangelical Christians in Latin America have assumed an attitude of polarization, emphasizing sometimes evangelization (preaching and proclamation) and sometimes social responsibility (prophetic denunciation and service). This polarization is not right, because both complete each other in preaching and living the gospel.

To preach the gospel means to announce good news, to announce the facts concerning the past, especially the death and resurrection of Christ, two events that were observed by eyewitnesses. The only Christ to preach and proclaim is the Christ we find in the Bible, the historical Jesus confirmed by the testimony of the Old Testament prophets and the apostles in the New Testament. This Christ, the Son of God, is the only one who can fill the existential emptiness of all social classes. Jesus Christ can give life to those who are dying from hunger, and can bring justice with peace to each activity of our everyday routine.

Social responsibility means having a heart that cries along with creation—a cry of compassion, a cry of identification. The church was born in a context of social responsibility; that is what we read in the apostles' letters (Ephesians 2:10) and in the book of Acts. The members of the New Testament church rescued such values as dignity, freedom, peace, justice, solidarity and love. They announced the Good News and, at the same time, their community lifestyle promoted general welfare (Acts 2:42-47). People were saved and healed, attitudes toward property and wealth were redirected, church leaders suffered a terrible persecution from the hegemonic secular and religious powers. Jesus was the pattern that guided them, as we can see from Luke 4:18-19.

We have seen an increase in the number of Latin American evangelical leaders committed to an understanding of the holistic mission of the church. These leaders are better able to see people in the totality of their physical, emotional, spiritual, cultural, political, economic and environmental needs.

The incarnational way is the answer for the Latin American evangelical church. Jesus Christ must be the pattern for the way we do mission. We have to look to Christ's message, lifestyle and mission strategy, to perceive the way Christ shows a genuine interest in other people's lives. This is our privilege, our responsibility, our life. Being rich, Jesus decided to become poor; being God, Jesus became a human being. Jesus' life shows us an attitude of renunciation as we face the challenge of the modern world's human needs—the simple needs for bread and a home, but also the complex needs facing the Latin American social reality.

The Holy Spirit invites us to open our eyes to recognize mission dimensions and challenges in the Latin American context—urban and rural, secular and religious. God has called us to lead lives of service so that God's love will reach the world. Latin America is known by its great inequalities: our societies suffer from unemployment, foreign debt and dependence on the First World; corruption takes the money that should be used for public health and education; more and more of our children die every day. God put us in this continent to answer to the realities of our time. We are called to change the reality we live in. We are called to be salt and light in the world. This means joining the fight for a world that is less cruel and unfair, a world with structures that are less sinful and less tyrannical. A holistic ministry is a way to change the present situation—the status quo—and organize it into a "new society" where signs of the kingdom of God appear.

HOLISTIC MINISTRY: WHAT WE ARE DOING IN THE CONTEXT

It is good to see that the church has developed in this field, in spite of the many difficulties of practicing a holistic attitude in the preaching of the gospel, the social responsibility of the church, the knowledge of the Bible and the worship of God. We can see this in all of the case studies.

To better analyze the practice of the cases, I would like to follow five approaches to social change proposed by Frances O'Gorman in her book *Charity and Change* (Melbourne: World Vision Australia, 1992). Dr. O'Gorman has long experience helping people on the mountains and *favelas* (slums) of Rio de Janeiro. She created a model with five different approaches that shows a life-changing process in society. The following presents the analysis outcome.

1. *Band-Aid* (reach out): Give a fish.
2. *Ladder* (catch up): Teach how to fish and give a rod.
3. *Patchwork* (patch up): Upgrade local fishing techniques and practices.
4. *Beehive* (honeycomb): Support grassroots movements claiming the right to a fair share of the fishing business.
5. *Beacon* (transform): Find a new basis for labor-life relationships beyond fisheries.

All the cases presented in this book exhibit the first three approaches. Some of them achieve the fourth approach, looking for the fulfillment of basic human needs for individuals and for society as a whole. There is one case that attempts the fifth approach, but has not fully achieved it. Each case tries to find alternate solutions for the poor with whom they work.

In each approach we see in the cases—consciously or unconsciously, explicitly or implicitly—the projects have a vision that is linked to the vertical relationship with God. As we see in the chapter on the Redeemer Project in Brazil, the project workers desired to draw closer to Jesus in the spirit of Matthew 25; they understood that the street people's individual problems are not solely responsible for bringing bad consequences to society, but that social problems also decidedly affect individuals who have little opportunity to adapt to a competitive and unfair world.

While these organizations begin to practice their vision and to define their mission, trying to make a difference by helping people in their whole human needs, they go on to other changes. They search for a total transformation of social relations. A new person needs to live in a new society, and a new society needs new people to guide it according to the values of the kingdom of God.

Holistic Ministry: Different Continuities

The holistic ministries presented in the case studies have different continuities, that is, the groups represented have an ability to manage their projects in a different manner from those in other continents, because the Latin America reality is different, even among the different countries. For example, the cell groups project in Peru established a relationship with the church and society in general, which is a different approach from that of the Redeemer Project in Brazil, and different again from the project in Nicaragua.

Do we understand our context well enough to start a holistic Christian ministry that influences the power relations in our churches and in our cities? Does this holistic ministry contribute to changing the passivity of the Latin American citizen and the church attender or the believer? Are the holistic ministries changing the lives of Christians and the life of the evangelical church? The poverty of the discussions involving these themes shows clearly the lack of interest Latin American evangelicals have. Leaders want only to attract people "by creating news." Church leaders do not support ideas that serve to awaken Christians or make them think about fundamental questions. A "dechristianization of Christ" exists. Christ is not the focus anymore; the focus is on the leader's strength, charisma or way of managing things. People do not know the Word of God, the meaning of grace, faith, good deeds, the history of the church.

Do the case studies represent the Latin American church described above? If we simply say yes, we are presenting these experiences as methods without any underlying philosophy of faith, service, values—in short, without any ethics. If we simply say no, we are denying our principles, our history, our Christian vocation.

Our answer, therefore, must be balanced. As participants in the Latin America Consultation on Holistic Ministry, we have tried to identify ourselves with the holistic ministry of the church of Christ. We have emphasized the participation of people from different segments of society and different churches, supporting them in different communities and projects; but we have also worked in a way that teaches us how to make a difference in our countries, cities and communities.

We desire and have practiced an alternate proposal for the Latin American evangelical church and for committed Christians who live by the Christian principles of equality, solidarity, justice, peace and faith. These are fundamental values for a new order.

This chapter has been critical of the evangelical church in Latin America, but with only one purpose: to open new horizons. By being critical we do not mock the evangelical church, whether it is traditional, Pentecostal, neopentecostal or liberal. Our proposal is not linked to any kind of church as a human organization. Our proposal is to walk with Christ and to follow the example of the people who formed the apostolic church. They made a difference, and we want to do the same in the Latin American communities where God has placed us.

THEMES FOR A NEW AGENDA

I would like to leave some questions for our reflection.

* How are we, as an evangelical church living in a secular and Roman Catholic continent, announcing the Good News to the different segments of society?
* Are we prepared to break with the secularization, the popular urban religiosity and the traditional rural Catholicism that pervade our culture?
* Why do we enjoy preaching and proclamation more than service and prophetic denunciation?
* Why, in our social action, do we prefer to give the fish or to teach someone to fish, rather than to fight for people's rights or to motivate them to go beyond the fishing business?
* How can holistic ministries be self-sustaining? Are there options other than partnerships with the municipality or NGOs?

Here are some themes that I believe should be on the holistic ministry manager's agenda. To avoid projects that create dependence, the great challenge in modern holistic ministry management is to organize groups in a way that creates extra-political (or extra-ecclesiastical) institutions that will open space to a balanced development in the communities where the project is located and where there is participation by the people. So I would suggest that the projects we saw in the case studies include the following:

a. *People's organization and the creation of cooperatives*. It is necessary that people feel responsible and able to change their lives, but they cannot compete with the financial and multinational enterprises by themselves. For any kind of cooperative, there should be medium-term planning that shows the people the possibility of economic viability. The small home enterprise, the family industry, the home kitchen garden, the wood and handcrafts production are all initiatives that can receive support and motivation, giving everyone the opportunity to participate in the decision-making and the profits. The creation of cooperatives is particularly interesting in the field of education, because it is an area generally neglected by the government.

b. *Quality programs in the projects.* Without sophistication and with low cost, it is possible to improve working conditions and increase internal and external funding, helping professionals, students and people in general. If there are medium or large enterprises in town, it is possible to work with business people who will act as consultants, helping the community through partnership.

c. *Community funds and managing the budgets.* This point is related to point a above. It is necessary to identify business opportunities, create associations and transform people into partners and controllers. Managing the budget can lower expenses and control investments according to the community's interests.

d. *Social programs.* Education and health programs, and those oriented toward children and women, must always have the interaction of community discussions and decisions through councils in the small projects or bigger organizations. Evangelization programs must have a strategy for each context, with an awareness of our Catholic and secular society that already knows some themes from Christian religiosity.

e. *Economic-social-participative projection.* A projection will help communities be prepared for the transformation.

f. *Qualification and training.* Knowledge is essential for everyone, but especially for the managers and teams because they will be responsible for a work of quality, a holistic quality.

REFERENCES

Couto, Alva. 1993. Ponencia "Mission y dessarollo comunitario integra," CLADE III, Tercer Congreso Latinoamericano de Evangelizacion, Quito 1992, Fraternidad Teologica Latinoamericana, pp. 606-618.

Couto, Alva. Ponencia "Evangelizacion y Responsabilidad Social," Congresso Nacional da Associacao Evangelica Brasileira (AEVB), Brasilia (DF), Julho 1994.

Escobar, Samuel. 1985. *Evangello y Realidad Social (Ensayos)*. Lima: Ediciones Presencia.

Gomes, Wadislau Martins. 1985. *Sal da Terra em Terra dos Brasis*. Refugio Editora Ltda., Primeira Edicao.

Quiroz, Pedro Arana. 1988. *Providencia y Revolucion*, Segunda Edicion. Grand Rapids, USA: Subcommission Literatura Cristiana.

Quiroz, Pedro Arana y Victor Arroyo. Novembro de 1988. *Llamados a servir*, Segunda Edicion. Lima: Ediciones Presencia.

Stott, John R.W. 1981. *Contracultura Crista*, Primeira Edicao. ABU Editora.

11
Holistic mission in theological perspective

C. René Padilla

If these case studies show anything, they show that healthy church growth is closely connected with the practice of holistic mission. As with the human body, so also with the church: not every kind of growth is healthy. Cancer, for instance, is nothing but an inordinate, and therefore undesirable, multiplication of cells. In the same way, a unilateral emphasis on one aspect of growth may result in unhealthy church growth, with the possibility that the church misses its role in relation to God's purpose for God's people.

HOLISTIC CHURCH GROWTH

At the beginning of the eighties Orlando E. Costas noticed the "extraordinary interest" that, in the face of the growing phenomenon of secularization, church leaders from all denominations had in church growth. Costas believed this concern should be biblically oriented, since "without an adequate understanding of what is growth itself and how it takes place in life, it is not possible to understand its nature and dynamics in the church nor to see the disorder that it causes."[1] To this end he suggested a model of holistic growth which would take into account three qualities derived from the nature of the church and four dimensions related to the church's reality as a faith community.

The qualities of growth

Taking as his starting point the nature of the church as the community of the Spirit, the body of Christ, and the people of God, Costas proposed that the criterion to evaluate the growth of the church has to be theological. From God's triune nature Costas derived three qualities of holistic growth: *spirituality* (referring to the inspiration and motivation of the Spirit in the growth), *incarnation* (referring to the way in which Jesus' compassion toward the harassed and helpless multitudes is made present in the growth), and *fidelity* (referring to the extent to which the growth reflects God's purpose for God's people).

The dimensions of growth

From the life and mission of the church as a faith community, Costas derived four dimensions of growth:

* ❖ *Numerical growth.* This dimension of growth oftentimes becomes the center of all the efforts made by the experts in "church growth." To justify their position they appeal to those texts in the Acts of the Apostles that refer to the multiplication of believers in the primitive church (see 2:47, 4:4, 5:14, 6:7,12:24, 19:20). It is questionable to assume that these texts provide an adequate basis for a unilateral emphasis on this dimension of growth. This does not deny, however, the importance of the reproduction of believers and churches as "a fundamental aspect of the church's being," since the church is called to spread throughout all nations and all cultures. As Costas put it, the church "as people on the march, will not be able to reach her goal until all humanity has had a reasonable opportunity to listen and to respond to the gospel."[2]

* ❖ *Organic growth.* Looking inside the church, it is necessary to pay attention to the development of the system of mutual relations in the faith community. According to Costas, this dimension includes such aspects of the life of the church as

"her form of government, her financial structure, her leadership, the sort of activities in which she invests time and resources, and her [worship] celebration."[3] It poses, among other things, the challenge of the contextualization of the church in a specific historical situation, with the view of becoming a true community with local roots.

* *Conceptual growth.* The church grows in "the intelligence of the faith" when it grows in "the degree of the awareness of its existence and purpose, its understanding of the Christian faith, its knowledge of the sources of this faith (Scripture), its interaction with the history of this faith, and its understanding of the world around it."[4] This knowledge is closely related to the discernment of the place of the church in society, a discernment that requires the consideration of concrete reality in a spirit of prayer and in light of the Word of God.

* *Diaconal growth.* Finally, Costas proposed that healthy church growth includes diaconal or incarnational growth, that is, "the intensity of the service that the church offers to the world as a concrete sign of God's redemptive love." According to Costas, without this service the church loses authenticity and credibility, since "only to the extent that its vocation of love and service becomes visible and concrete can it expect to be heard and respected."[5]

The awakening of the evangelical social conscience

Costas' article on the dimensions of holistic church growth, synthesized in the foregoing paragraphs, illustrates the awakening of the evangelical social conscience which took place around the world beginning in the sixties.[6] As was the case with various authors associated with the *Fraternidad Teológica Latinoamericana* (Latin American Theological Fraternity), Costas, in his effort to articulate an evangelical missiology which would overcome the polarization between evangelism and social responsibility, came to the concept of holistic mission. For this purpose he followed the way of theological reflection on those elements that he regarded as essential for the church to grow according to its divine nature, that is, as the community of the Spirit, the body of Christ, and the people of God:

> As the community of the Spirit, it should grow in holiness and communion. As the body of Christ, it should grow in apostolicity (mission) and unity. As the people of God, it should grow in fidelity to God's work in history and in the celebration of his wonderful works.[7]

In agreement with this purpose, Costas proposed a "holistic theory" of church growth in the following terms:

> It is a process of holistic and normal expansion that can and must be expected for the life and mission of the church as the community of the Spirit, the body of Christ, and the people of God.[8]

Costas' response to the reductionism of the "evangelists" and the reductionism of the "social activists" was not a denial of the validity of evangelism or of service or social action. Instead, it was a renewed emphasis on growth as a complex phenomenon which combines the various qualities and dimensions that have been mentioned:

> It may be said that the church grows holistically when it receives new members, expands internally, deepens her knowledge of the faith, and serves the world. But it grows qualitatively when it reflects spirituality, incarnation, and faithfulness in each dimension.[9]

With this model of holistic and qualitative church growth, Costas laid down the basis for a tool to evaluate the life and mission of the churches, taking into account the relation between the qualities and the dimensions of growth.

This approach by the Puerto Rican missiologist is a valuable corrective to the common tendency to reduce church growth to numerical growth. This model emphasizes the need to place theological criteria ahead of mere numbers in evaluating the growth of the church.

What follows is an attempt to use this tool to evaluate a few cases of holistic mission developed in Latin America. From the start we admit the limited character of this evaluation, due to the lack of data that we would need to accomplish our task more thoroughly. Nevertheless, we hope this attempt will demonstrate the close relation between holistic mission and holistic—as well as quality—church growth.

EVALUATING THE CASES OF HOLISTIC MISSION

All of these cases illustrate a search which in the last few years has been advancing in evangelical circles, especially in the Two-Thirds World: the search for models of holistic mission that might clearly show to society God's love in word and action. Just as there are no perfect Christians, neither are there mission models that would show an absolute correlation between all the qualities and all the dimensions of holistic church growth. Every model can use improvement. Nevertheless, what follows is evidence of how much we have advanced along the road of missionary obedience in these last few years.

In this evaluation we adopt two approaches. In both approaches the evaluation is made on the basis of the criteria for holistic church growth mentioned above. But in the first approach we look at only one case (the Redeemer Project in Curitiba, Brazil), whereas in the second we consider all the cases as a whole and arrive at certain conclusions regarding the holistic mission represented by those cases. With the first approach we wish to illustrate the way in which the various dimensions and qualities of holistic growth are combined in the evaluation of a given ministry. With the second approach we wish to show the similarities and differences resulting from the way in which the dimensions and qualities of holistic growth are combined in the various projects.

Evaluation of the Redeemer Project in Curitiba, Brazil

The number of people who have been transformed inside out and have joined the church because of this project is apparently significant. Conversions to Christ have occurred not only among "street people"—the program's primary target (including the first man contacted on the street at the beginning of the ministry)—but also among the personnel of the public service staff (including the former director of municipal social service), as well as among the volunteers. The official position regarding the central aim of evangelization is clear:

> Our first priority and commitment is to proclaim the gospel of our Lord Jesus Christ. Coming to faith and repentance in light of this gospel is the only way for people to be truly free.

1. What ensures the quality of *numerical growth* resulting from that evangelization, nonetheless, is the emphasis on the work of the Holy Spirit; on entering into the world of the socially marginalized, "the poorest of the poor"; on coming close to Jesus "in the spirit of Matthew 25"; and on the coherence between the work and God's purpose in using God's people as salt and light.

2. Numerical growth goes hand in hand with *organic growth*. This becomes evident, first, in the articulation of God's love in terms of a missionary project appropriate to an urban situation where an increasing number of people live on the street as a result of current economic conditions. In addition to taking advantage of the human and economic resources of the churches and the secular social service institutions, the Redeemer Project emphasizes elements of the Christian faith that make it an instrument specially apt to reach those on the margins: solidarity with the poor, a simple lifestyle, community life, stewardship of material goods, love expressed in service, the dignity of people who are made in God's image and the prophetic note. It is also surprising that the greatest financial support for this ministry comes from a local church, which shows that the congregation has reached a high degree of unity in their understanding of the life and mission of the church.

3. Another aspect of holistic growth that receives attention in the Redeemer Project is *conceptual growth*. Many of the practices that are part of the participants' lives are related to this aspect. For instance, the "periods of silence, prayer and reflection" at the beginning and end of the activities in the Living Center; the development of "a more holistic theology" as volunteers return to their churches after participating in the project's ministries; and the effort to root the project's vision "in the examples of the church's

past, starting with Christ's ministry and drawing from the Acts of the Apostles, the early church fathers, the Christian mystics, the Reformation, pietism, evangelicalism and pentecostalism." There is a clear vision of forming leaders whose presentation of the gospel integrates their context of pious personal ethics with active involvement, and fosters a personal encounter with the Father.

4. Finally, the Redeemer Project points to *diaconal growth*. The project started "without the support of the community or the local churches, or even a well-structured plan," as a result of the vision from a youth group of a church in crisis, with a modest "relief" ministry—food, clothes and a bathing area—to marginalized people. Since then it has grown steadily and has become a multiphase ministry which seeks solutions for this abandoned sector of the population, in collaboration not just with the churches but also with public and private institutions of social welfare. The diaconal growth is evident also in the aspiration to increase the ministry in the near future to include mentally disturbed women and terminal AIDS patients.

All the dimensions of growth include the features of spirituality, incarnation and fidelity, which ensure the health of holistic growth by means of the Redeemer Project.

Evaluation of the Cases as a Whole

The numerical dimension

It is quite obvious that in all these cases of holistic mission the aim of increasing the number of believers is present; some also aim to form new churches. None of these cases leaves room to think that the mission agents have to choose between evangelization and service. On the contrary, the symbiotic integration of evangelization with the agricultural program explains at least in part the surprising numerical growth of the Assemblies of God in northwestern Nicaragua, and the community projects promoted by CORCRIDE have contributed a great deal to the numerical expansion of the churches in the southern province of Choluteca, Honduras.

The analysis of the cases presented here leads us to the following conclusions regarding the numerical dimension of growth:

1. Every human need can be used as an insertion point for the message of the gospel into the lives of individuals or groups. Consequently, there are no fixed rules regarding what comes first—evangelization or service.

The World Vision project in Cali, Colombia, began with the physical needs of women determined to improve life conditions for their families. Their emphasis on human dignity gave these women a new sense of personal identity and led them to accept their role as agents of change as well as followers of Jesus Christ. The BEM ministry in Sabinópolis, Brazil, started with a center for the care of children affected by hunger, malnutrition and homelessness.

The Evangelical Hospital in Siguatepeque, Honduras, started with an exclusively evangelistic emphasis in which social work, including health, was conceived only as a means of providing the space for communicating the gospel. The greatest social impact Food for the Hungry had at Juntavi, Bolivia, came about when the Christian agronomist representing it went to live in the community and began with a weekly prayer and Bible study meeting in his home. The Redeemer Project in Curitiba started with a church youth group that was looking for greater Christian authenticity by serving the poorest of the poor.

One of the characteristics of holistic mission is the freedom to start the task in each situation, not according to pre-established formulas, but according to guidance by God's Spirit. The best theological support for such freedom is the assurance that God's kingdom embraces the totality of reality. Consequently, there is nothing that lies beyond the reach of God's redemptive purpose. People's material or economic, physical, psychological, sociopolitical and spiritual needs are all within God's realm of action; they represent spheres of human life where God calls people, on an individual and community level, to submit to God and experience God's transforming power. From this all-encompassing vision of the kingdom comes what Emilio Castro has called "missionary freedom, the capacity to respond in love to the need of all."[10]

2. Service projects do not need any other justification than that derived from God's love but, according to the situation, they fulfill various objectives related to the announcement of the Good News of Jesus Christ.

In some cases, service has demolished the barriers of religious prejudice and has opened a road to the announcement of the gospel in an adverse context. This is particularly important in Latin America, where the prejudices of Constantinian Roman Catholic Christianity dominate the religious environment, as we can easily infer from the case studies. Over and over, service has become the means to plow the ground to sow the seed of the Word, because it has shown that what moves Christians in their social relations is not a desire for profit but love for their neighbor. Several of the cases explicitly mentioned that the social help projects have made the Christian message credible, no doubt because they have demonstrated Christian love "not . . . with words or tongue but with actions and in truth" (1 John 3:18).

The Consultation on Evangelization and Social Responsibility held at Grand Rapids, U.S.A., in 1982, suggested that the evangelistic and social responsibilities of the church are related to one another in three ways: 1) social action is a consequence of evangelism, since "evangelism is the means by which God brings people to new birth, and their new life manifests itself in the service of others";[11] 2) social action is a bridge to evangelism, a way "to break down prejudice and suspicion, open closed doors, and gain a hearing for the gospel";[12] 3) action accompanies evangelization as its partner, since "both issue from the lordship of Jesus, for he sends us out into the world both to preach and to serve."[13]

Each of the cases illustrates at least one of these three relations more or less emphatically, according to the situation. Instead of attempting to understand the type of relation between evangelism and social action present in each case, we should recognize that we can distinguish the elements of this two-fold Christian responsibility from one another to a certain extent, but we must not separate them. They are so closely interrelated that it would be more appropriate to describe them as two forms of Christian witness in symbiotic or complementary relationship to each other. There is no genuine evangelism without a social dimension, nor is there truly Christian social responsibility without an evangelistic dimension.

Nevertheless, the distinction between the two forms of witness may help us avoid the tendency to emphasize one while forgetting the other: the "evangelicals" announce the Good News while neglecting their social responsibility; the "social activists" do social action while ignoring the announcement of the gospel. The Lord's call is to a holistic mission in which the constant aim is to bear witness to Christ in both word and deed—sharing with the needy the Bread of Life along with the daily bread.

3. *The message of the gospel is inseparable from the messenger's life.*

In several of the projects a true integration between evangelism and life witness has been achieved; proclaiming the gospel is not an activity but a lifestyle articulated by words and action. The modeling of values related to the equality of men and women in the lives of those in charge of World Vision's project in Colombia, for instance, was decisive in evangelizing women at Aguablanca.

4. *Holistic mission fulfills its objective of witness to the gospel more fully when church leaders are committed to evangelism and service.*

A good example of this is the BEM ministry in Sabinópolis, Brazil, where the project leaders are also church leaders, so that both the project and the churches complement each other. For the Office for Social Advancement and Development in Barranquilla, Colombia, to achieve its function in microenterprise development, it was necessary for the church leaders to have a change of mind about holistic mission. A factor that has resulted in the surprising evangelistic impact by the Assemblies of God in Nicaragua has been the pastors' participation in the work of the Social Development Institute, and sometimes in the coordination of the promotion of farming. No one can exaggerate the importance of leaders being active in service as an essential aspect of the life and mission of the church.

5. *Holistic mission keeps the church from becoming a mere religious sect, making possible a wide participation by "secular" people in evangelism and service activities.*

In this sense I would stress the ministry of the Office for Social Advancement and Development in Barranquilla, Colombia, whose aim is the spiritual, economic and social development of individuals, groups and communities. The local churches provide volunteers and space for the office and training classes, and the social project works with groups of believers and unbelievers, opening up the chance for the former to share their faith with the latter. As a result, "microentrepreneurs have become witnesses to God's love and power," thus multiplying the number of people who share their faith with neighbors and friends. The churches are showing in a practical way "that one can love and share to survive," and enabling laypeople to make use of their administrative and service gifts in the cause of the gospel.

The organic dimension

The cases show that holistic mission not only contributes to the numerical growth of the church, but also contributes to the church's growth as a contextualized Christian community in a particular situation. In this sense we suggest the following conclusions:

1. Holistic mission helps develop local leaders who rise from the grassroots.

It is not surprising that when Food for the Hungry discontinued its support for the project in Juntavi, Bolivia, the community was willing to carry on the work of community development and the training of disciples: it counted on leaders committed to God's service. At Aguablanca, Colombia, two years after World Vision's work with women had begun, those who had participated in the first training groups supported the program's activities and were recognized as leaders in other sectors of the community. In Sabinópolis, Brazil, the social projects of the Evangelical Missionary Pentecostal Church are now directed by a new generation trained by the church. In Barranquilla, Colombia, there are Christians who, as a result of the ministry of the Office for Social Advancement and Development, have gained confidence through their participation in microenterprise groups and have become leaders in their community and effective evangelists.

110

All these projects prove that the key to producing results of permanent value are not development programs as such, but the development of persons, of leaders. In John M. Perkins' words, "developing creative leaders is both the most essential and the most difficult part of Christian community development."[14]

2. Holistic mission makes possible the full participation of Christians in the people's struggles and problems, as well as in their aspirations and hopes.

Christians participate in an important activity organized by the city government in Aguablanca, Colombia. The Redeemer Project has vital contact with entities working for the public well-being and with the Federal Social Bank and the Creativity Center of Curitiba. The churches in northwestern Nicaragua promote crops of basic grains and family plots, and support local authorities in projects for the common good, such as the construction of schools and latrines. All of these are encouraging signs of a new way to live out the Christian faith and to be a witness to Jesus Christ in the world. They show that Christians do not remain foreign to the felt needs of the people around them. It is not surprising that with all of this the image of the church as a religious sect aiming at life beyond this world is slowly being replaced by the image of the church as a community that honors the Son of Man, who did not come to be served "but to serve, and to give his life as a ransom for many" (Mark 10:45).

3. Holistic mission makes the church a true agent of complete transformation, and is recognized as such by the lay community.

In the case of the ministry in Aguablanca, Colombia, participation by the women in the community groups has allowed them to gain self-confidence to such an extent that now they are preparing themselves to achieve changes in the political arena. In El Carmen de Bolivar, Colombia, one of the Christian microentrepreneurs was elected as a member of the city council in recognition of his contribution to society. In these and in many other places Christians committed to holistic mission come into contact with the reality around them and are the salt of the earth and the light of the world.

4. Holistic mission provides the church with an economic basis for its ministry.

In Barranquilla, Colombia, the microenterprise program sponsored by the Office for Social Advancement and Development produces a significant increase in the income of the churches involved in the program. In northwestern Nicaragua, those who benefit from the Social Development Institute of the Assemblies of God are committed to giving one-tenth of their crops to the committee in charge of the community preschool. These two examples show the potential holistic mission has for churches to cover their own economic needs and at the same time demonstrate their mission of service to the community.

5. Parachurch entities find their reason for existence to the extent that they foster the church's organic growth and empower local churches for holistic mission.

Nearly all the projects are sponsored by parachurch entities—whether national or international, denominational or interdenominational. On the one hand, they show the importance of these structures as specialized ministries that take advantage of human resources (e.g., professionals) from various churches for the sake of holistic mission. In several cases, these structures were the means God used to bring about a more holistic view of the gospel among the local Christians. On the other hand, some of the projects showed an inherent danger the parachurch structures have of isolating themselves from the churches to carry out their programs, instead of empowering the churches to fulfill their holistic mission in their own community. As Howard A. Snyder affirms,

> Whereas the church itself is part of the new wine of the gospel, all para-church structures are wineskins—useful, at times indispensable, but also subject to wear and decay.[15]

The conceptual dimension

The cases under consideration show, in general terms, that the holistic approach to mission provides the very best means of responding to the conceptual (or theological) dimension of growth.

Thus, from an analysis of these cases we arrive at the following conclusions:

1. Holistic mission presupposes the formation of ecclesiastical leaders who have an ample vision of life and church mission.

The teaching given by the church leaders—whether good, fair or poor—determines to a large extent the way in which the church they lead relates to the surrounding world. A common problem in Latin America is that many evangelical church leaders have been trained with a limited (that is to say, "spiritualistic") vision of the gospel and the mission of the church in the world. They reflect what Jose Miguez Bonino has called, "the model of the American evangelicalism of the 'second awakening': individualistic, Christo-logical-soteriological in a basically subjective key, with emphasis on sanctification."[16] Consequently these churches maintain a strong emphasis on a "separation from the world" that gives them a sec-tarian slant and limits their role as agents of holistic transformation.

It is not an accident that in several of the case studies reference is made to the change of mind that the church leaders have experi-enced, opening the way for the insertion of these churches into the secular community. When the leaders have a biblical vision of the church in the world, non-Christians can expect to see it not "as a religion or just another sect, but . . . as a community of people who live out and share the love of God," as occurred in Barranquilla, Colombia, thanks to the ministry of the Office for Social Advance-ment and Development." From this perspective we can understand why one of the first tasks undertaken by this Office was to share with church leaders the "vision of . . . holistic work for the exten-sion of the gospel."

2. The needs of the poor and the marginalized provide the opportunity to teach to the entire local church, theoretically and practically, "the whole purpose of God" for creation and humankind, and the place of the church in relation to that purpose.

If we reduce the church's task to the verbal communication of the "plan of salvation" through Jesus Christ, it is enough to provide believers with a simple method to accomplish that communication.

The "four spiritual laws" is an example of this. But if the church's task is to witness to "the whole purpose of God"—using Paul's expression in Acts 20:27 (TEV)—for creation and humankind, then training to transmit a doctrinal formula is totally insufficient. For the teaching of the whole gospel and for authentic evangelism, recovering Jesus' pedagogy—the pedagogy in which theory and practice, as well as doctrine and spirituality, are united in the actual practice of holistic mission—is essential. By participating in holistic mission, believers learn that

> We proclaim salvation in Christ. That means salvation in his body, salvation in his kingdom, salvation in his plan to trans-form all reality. So any word that announces the gospel is an entry point into the total kingdom; if not it is not an authentic proclamation of the gospel.[17]

3. Holistic mission provides the context for the conversion to Jesus Christ not to be merely a religious experience but a total reorientation of life—a conversion to God's kingdom and God's justice.

From the perspective of God's kingdom, salvation in Christ is not merely a subjective religious experience, separate from life in history, but a reorientation of all of life toward the fulfillment of God's purpose in human life and in creation. In light of God's kingdom, the following elements are most important for church growth:

- ❖ The emphasis of the Christian Social Project in Aguablanca, Colombia, in internalizing the values of the gospel and in developing a conscience that turned the women of the community into agents of change among their families and communities.
- ❖ The similar emphasis of BEM in Sabinópolis, Brazil, on the priority of the family, and the change in the ways the "people deal with their day-to-day problems and their relationships with family members, neighbors and society in general."
- ❖ The teaching of the Bible that the Redeemer Project offers to the street people of Curitiba, Brazil, combined with vocational and professional training programs.

❖ The concern by the leaders of the Evangelical Hospital in Siguatepeque, Honduras, to make a contribution "in transformation and biblical reflection processes."

The diaconal dimension

We can see in all these cases that, to some extent, the ministries involved believe service is an integral part of the mission of the church. They do not reduce mission to merely verbalizing the gospel, nor do they assume that Christians have to choose between evangelization and social responsibility. The analysis of these cases takes us to the following conclusions regarding the diaconal growth of the church:

1. Each human need is an opportunity for service.

The projects described represent an ample range of services: from promoting new farming techniques to providing a place for bathing, from child care to developing community gardens, from conscientizing about the place of women in society to assisting microenterprises. Each form of service becomes a means whereby God's love becomes historically visible. Each form of service is a sign of God's kingdom, which became history in Jesus Christ.

Most of the projects are related to rural communities. Others are directly related to the severe problem in Latin America posed by the internal migrations from country to city. The latter communities are samples of the thousands and millions of migrants who constitute the belts of poverty around our cities. Never before have the evangelical churches been confronted by a challenge of such magnitude; never before have they had such a great opportunity to grow in the experience of service in the name of Jesus Christ.

2. Service is better if it is integrated with the other aspects of holistic mission, starting with the gospel of God's kingdom. Such integration frees the church to cooperate with secular entities for the common good, without neglecting Christian witnessing.

Although in all these cases service occupies an important place, it is obvious that only some of them have achieved the full integration of service with the other aspects of holistic mission. Integration is much more evident in those cases where from the beginning there was a recognition that all areas of human life are interrelated, that all can be equally transformed by God's power, and that all are therefore mission fields.

In other cases service appears to be merely a spearhead for the verbal announcement of the gospel. When Christians understand that God's kingdom is the new order which emerged in history through Jesus Christ, and that it embraces the totality of history and creation, then everything they are and all they do and say take on new meaning as a witness to that new order. With this understanding, their central preoccupation is the exaltation of the King-Servant as Lord over all of life and history, and each aspect of holistic mission has equal testimonial value as the others. This vision frees them to cooperate with any human project—of government or private entities—that fosters justice, peace and the integrity of creation, as long as there is no compromise of Christian witness.

The qualities of growth

Spirituality, incarnation and faithfulness provide the principles of theological critique to assess church growth. Let us briefly evaluate the projects in light of these criteria.

1. Spirituality

Most of the cases do not contain data for judging to what extent the project leaders are conscious of the presence and operation of the Holy Spirit in all the dimensions of church growth. It is possible that some of them would relate the work of the Spirit exclusively to numerical growth. The fact is, however, that several of the cases do not even mention the Spirit. In one case the Spirit is recognized in the development of "a new generation of leaders with a renewed vision of the holistic work of the church" (the Office for Social Advancement and Development). Another case refers to "our great need of the power and anointing of the Holy Spirit to confront and triumph over the powers of this world, both visible and invisible" (the Redeemer Project).

2. Incarnation

All the projects described are directed at the poorest sectors of the population: rural farmers; city slum dwellers; street people; refugees; families with scarce resources; and single or abandoned mothers and widows. In some of these projects the intent is evident to serve as a witness to Christ and be present amid crowds that are "harassed and helpless, like sheep without a shepherd" (Matthew 9:36). The case of the project in Juntavi, Bolivia, highlights "the integration of the church in the daily life of the community." In the same project, the agronomist working for Food for the Hungry is a magnificent example of relocation. It leads us to John M. Perkins' affirmation:

> The incarnation is the ultimate relocation. Not only is the incarnation relocation; relocation is also incarnation. That is, not only did God relocate among us by taking the form of a man, but when a fellowship of believers relocates into a community, Christ incarnate invades that community. Christ, as his body, as his church, comes to dwell there.[18]

3. Faithfulness

God has not called us to be successful but to be faithful in everything we are and do. In the final analysis, only God can judge faithfulness in the performance of the task entrusted to us as God's people. Nevertheless, we can ask ourselves to what extent the church growth resulting from the programs that have been described are a response to God's action and purpose in history. I propose that to answer this question we adopt the criterion suggested by Perkins:

> Whether we take the gospel to the poor . . . is not an incidental side issue; it is a revealing test of the church's faithfulness to Christ's mission.[19]

From this perspective, the road of faithfulness is the road of a holistic mission that announces good news to the poor and proclaims the day of the Lord, Jubilee, the kingdom of God that in Jesus Christ broke into history, with all its sociopolitical and economic implications.

NOTES

1 Orlando E. Costas, "Dimensiones de crecimiento integral de la iglesia," in *Misión* 1:2 (July-September 1982:9).

2 Ibid., p. 13.

3 Ibid.

4 Ibid.

5 Ibid.

6 On this awakening, see *Texts on Evangelical Social Ethics 1974-1983* and *How Evangelicals Endorsed Social Responsibility*, C. René Padilla and Chris Sugden, editors (Nottingham: Grove Books Limited, 1985), and "La Fraternidad Teológica Latinoamericana y la responsabilidad social de la Iglesia," *Vienticinco años de teología evangelíca latinoamericana*, C. René Padilla, editor (Buenos Aires: FTL, 1995), pp. 87-100.

7 Costas, pp. 11-12.

8 Ibid., p. 12.

9 Ibid., p. 14.

10 Emilio Castro, *Sent Free* (Grand Rapids: Wm. B. Eerdmans Publishing Co., 1985), p. 87.

11 CRESR, *Evangelism and Social Responsibility: An Evangelical Commitment* (Exeter: The Paternoster Press, 1982), p. 21.

12 Ibid., p. 22.

13 Ibid., p. 23.

14 John M. Perkins, *Beyond Charity: The Call to Christian Community Development* (Grand Rapids: Baker Book House, 1993), p. 74.

15 Howard A. Snyder, *The Community of the King* (Downers Grove: InterVarsity Press, 1977), p. 159.

16 Jose Miguez Bonino, *Faces of Latin American Evangelicalism* (Grand Rapids: Wm. B. Eerdmans Publishing Co., 1996), p. 40.

17 Castro, p. 101.

18 John M. Perkins, *With Justice for All* (Ventura: Regal Books, 1982), p. 88.

19 Ibid.

12
The cases from a management perspective

Javier Mayorga

The common denominator in these case studies is that the people involved strived to do things right; they sought results and to make good use of resources. It is our desire to be good stewards. Nevertheless, the task of administering holistic projects is complex. There is constant pressure to achieve more with less in an ever-changing environment.

As a result of the economic crisis in which we live, Latin America faces a social situation that demands strategic responses from the church and other institutions. There must be effective solutions to the problems we face.

Through holistic ministries we seek to bring about permanent change in people by employing the values of the kingdom of God. We strive for holistic transformation. To achieve conscientious administration in this kind of project, administration must be holistic. It must combine Christian principles and ethics with management techniques that are appropriate to our ministries.

A Christian focus is a constant in the projects presented in this book. We can easily observe that all of the projects offer opportunities for the people they seek to serve to know Jesus and to grow spiritually. In management terms, however, we find a series of activities directed at achieving maximum operational efficiency. What is lacking is a focus that defines and develops more effective ministries. As Christians we must strive for more than operational efficiency; we must seek a quality strategic ministry.

The management styles in the cases differ greatly. In the Redeemer Project in Brazil, there is a very flexible and spontaneous model; other cases illustrate a very institutionalized model, such as the BEM project in Brazil. This is logical, as there are many distinct variables from one project to another. Independent of the kind of project, however, there are certain management elements to consider. For the duration of the project, it is important that administration be an effective instrument in the fight for sustainable development and for meeting the project's basic needs.

Among these elements we can consider the following: human resources, the organization, sustainable systems, impact indicators, institutional change and strategic vision. The first five are key elements for every project and the last constitutes the connecting thread that drives all of our actions. We must develop our strategic vision to provide direction, coherence and orientation to our actions.

Let us analyze in detail each of these elements in the case studies, to show their interconnectedness and to develop effective organizational management.

HUMAN RESOURCES

All of the cases illustrate the relevancy and importance of human resources. It is a factor analyzed in each case. Knowing this, however, we must ask: Is it easy to find the ideal staff? No. It is something that is very difficult; it may be the most difficult task in administration.

The majority of the strategies used in the holistic projects involve people. One of the tensions that an organization must deal with is the question of whether to hire non-Christian personnel. The question is: How can we continue to actively provide a Christian witness in our ministry and still have staff who are not believers?

This is a situation dealt with in many different ways. There are those who opt for a radical position and do not even consider the possibility of hiring non-Christians. In this case, the results are not always what one would expect.

Another position reserves leadership positions for committed Christians, permitting non-Christians to occupy operational and technical staff positions. The difficulty in this situation comes from the pressures that exist in trying to find committed Christians for the key positions.

At the other extreme there is a position that does not differentiate between believers and nonbelievers. It assumes that "good" can be done by all, as related in the story of the Good Samaritan. This position has fewer followers.

There are other critical management issues related to human resources. These include securing adequate funds for staff training and providing opportunities for personal and professional fulfillment. The last issue presents us with the disjunction of how to provide personal opportunities without focusing all our energies on ourselves. These are difficult questions to answer, but these are the issues that are before us as administrators, to enable the worker to produce and feel motivated, trained and assured.

The most important actions we can point to in the management of human resources are:

Servant leadership

The best example of this kind of leadership comes from our Lord Jesus Christ. The model of Jesus' service is sacrificial, demonstrated by example. Translated to the management field, we would define servant leadership as actions that facilitate the conditions in which employees can achieve their best work. An essential element of this model is that we "preach" through our example.

The case of the cell groups in Peru provides us with a living example of this kind of leadership. This case study by Atilio Quintanilla describes how the cell groups are informal meetings of friends in a warm, friendly environment. In this setting the leader provides a short spiritual reflection, then they pray and share a simple snack. The people immediately sense the profound friendship, love and mutual support that is present among the group's members. Witnessing this expression of unity and acceptance, they, too, wish to be part of the group.

Staff training

The only way to secure the personnel we need and improve our services is through staff training. We must take into account that education is one of the most important motivations that we can provide.

Enrique Martinez highlights the importance of training in the case of the Evangelical Hospital in Siguatepeque. He mentions that training is one of the services the hospital offers. Through this training, the hospital has qualified staff who make an important contribution to the national health system. Today there are nurses, nurse auxiliaries and laboratory technicians who have been trained in the hospital and who now serve throughout Honduras.

The practice of prayer

The practice of prayer is a vital activity in the development of our ministry. Transforming this world is God's work; we are only collaborators in the process. From this point of view, the Holy Spirit is key to what we do and especially to what we achieve. Whatever strategy we employ is complementary to this work. As Paul states, "Not that we are competent in ourselves to claim anything for ourselves, but our competence comes from God" (2 Corinthians 3:5).

In the Food for the Hungry case in Bolivia, Ivan Delgado shows us the relevance the practice of prayer had in the life of Paz Gutiérrez, the community development worker. Gutiérrez began his ministry with fervent prayer for the community. The challenge to maintain this practice was great; initially, only one other Christian was there to pray with him.

ORGANIZATION

Organization is decisive in determining the participation of the people we seek to serve; our intention is that they be subjects—not objects—of the development process. This factor is important at different levels: in the community, in the project personnel who facilitate the processes in the community, and in the project institution (the local church, nongovernmental organizations, others).

The role of the community

Relief has its time and place; sustained over the long run it creates dependency. For this reason the design of the services should always consider the role of the community in the identification of its needs and the inclusion of local resources in the search for solutions.

Conscious and broad participation

To achieve the conscious and broad participation of the group, we should promote educational processes that strengthen democratic structures that are representative and flexible, able to respond to any context. This is much more feasible at the local level than within the institution.

In the case of Aguablanca in Colombia, presented by Débora de Arco, the role of the women and their broad participation contributed to the achievement of significant changes in their lives and the life of their community. The case study shows how the work groups provided an opportunity for women to become change agents for their families and communities.

Ownership of the processes

The case studies show how a process of training and decentralization that involves the community members contributes significantly to the continuity of the programs and their long-range impact. This is what we can observe in the case of the Food for the Hungry project in Juntavi, Bolivia. The different community committees assumed responsibility for the maintenance and management of irrigation systems, the community pharmacy and the distribution of piped water.

Legal registration

Three important aspects contribute to the consolidation of community groups: the opportunity for representation, their power and their legal situation. The need for legal registration has become much more important in recent years. One reason for this has been an insistence by agencies that they provide financial support through legally registered organizations. Legal registration also provides the means for a more permanent structure for the project. Among the cases presented here, CORCRIDE in Honduras demonstrates the importance of this registration.

SUSTAINABLE SYSTEMS

There are many reasons why the changes we seek to initiate in people and the environment do not continue. One reason our programs end is that we cannot secure the necessary resources to operate for the long term. Another cause is a community's dependence on our agencies. Other causes include the mismanagement of funds, bad decisions, lack of leadership development and weak organizations. In the analysis of the cases at least three aspects contribute significantly to the sustainability of ministry:

1. *Diversifying financial sources.* Every day, projects face the need to raise funds, especially from local sources. Whenever possible, services provided by a project should be self-financing.

2. *Integrity in the administration of funds.* This is important for the image of the organization, and for the confidence of the funding agencies as well as the community. It is very important that at the heart of the project there is a transparency in the management of financial resources. The following actions can help: implementing an accounting and auditing system according to generally accepted accounting principles, and offering frequent reports on the progress of the project and the use of funds. Among the reasons the Evangelical Hospital has been able to continue for almost fifty years has been its image of integrity and its diversification of revenue sources.

3. *Developing new leaders.* This is an essential skill in effective management. The constant improvement and continuity of programs depend to a great extent on the development of new leaders. Denise da Silva's chapter on BEM in Brazil shows that their experience with young people has been very beneficial. People have come up through their programs and are now project leaders.

IMPACT INDICATORS

We expect results from our work, and it is normal that others should expect to see results as well. We often neglect to take the time to develop indicators that enable us to measure, with objectivity, exactly what it is we are achieving. We should define the key indicators of our ministries, based on the long-range vision for the project, and the objectives and strategies that we elect to use.

Monitoring and evaluation

Many times it is difficult to measure how many of the changes we observe actually correspond to our actions and how many relate to other factors. This is why it is important that a project have clear objectives and establish a set of indicators to use in measuring the most important aspects of the project. This evaluation system should facilitate the monitoring of key aspects that permit frequent comparisons and in-depth evaluation over time.

Evaluation is one of the least-utilized management tools. This is probably due to the fact that it is difficult to define the indicators. In the case studies, it would appear that the indicator most clearly stated is the number of new Christians or converts. The project that shows the most effort in this area is the cell group project in Peru. In general, Christian organizations should do more to develop the capacity to objectively measure the results they are achieving.

ORGANIZATIONAL CHANGE

The environment in which holistic ministries are operating is now changing rapidly. For this reason the projects and the organizations that support them should develop the capability to readjust continually as the changes occur. Within the projects there should also be a continual search for ways to improve services.

Systematizing the experience

We should build on lessons learned and develop new actions. Evaluation and monitoring can be effective sources for feedback to process and analyze. The history of CORCRIDE in Honduras is a story of organizational change. The process began with the initiation of the project by a national relief and development organization. The combination of training, experience and reflection enabled the Christians in the region to become involved and eventually form CORCRIDE.

Kingdom values in practice

The best way to promote kingdom values is to put them into practice and model them in our organizations and projects. Justice, love, truth and all the values of the kingdom must be present in every action, with more intensity each day, among those we seek to serve. Perhaps this is the greatest challenge for a holistic ministry. In the case of the Redeemer Project in Brazil, as told by Claudio Oliver, we find a movement within the church that seeks to practice kingdom values by identifying with the poor of the city.

STRATEGIC THINKING

Without a well-defined work strategy, whatever we do will seem all right. However, our commitment to develop holistic ministries does not allow us to run that risk. We must develop management skills that enable us to implement ministries that are effective and that go beyond operational efficiency. Some of these skills include the following:

1. *Project design by stages.* Designing holistic projects in stages permits appropriate actions—according to the level of maturity achieved within the project—and at the same time minimizes the failures due to factors beyond our control. Normally there is an initial stage consisting of diagnosis, organization and motivation; a second stage of implementation and then the consolidation of achievements and the closing of the project. The Food for the Hungry project in Juntavi, Bolivia, illustrates these stages. It does not indicate, however, what to include in each stage, or how long each one should be.

2. *Constant self-criticism.* Constantly asking the basic questions about our ministry is a management skill that is very important to develop. What are we seeking to do with the community? How effective are our methods? How can we ensure

the continuity of the processes? How do the beneficiaries feel about the programs? Are there other means of support? These and many other questions arise in our daily pilgrimage. Food for the Hungry asks a fundamental question after four years in Juntavi: Should we continue with the "food for work" program? From that point the project changed radically.

3. *Long-range vision.* It is important that a project articulate a clear vision for where it would like to be in five years. The projects that have difficulty in establishing a vision have little possibility of making a substantial impact, and their survival is in jeopardy. Sooner or later, people without a vision perish.

4. *Appropriate strategies.* The strategies we use should be appropriate to the particular context in which we work. Many holistic projects end up with unwanted results because they used strategies that were not sensitive to the overall project environment. Many of the cases presented discuss the need to adopt strategies that are appropriate to the context, with the conviction that this sensitivity will achieve more results. Of these cases, the Office for Social Advancement and Development of Barranquilla, Colombia, opted to work with solidarity groups and community banks as a means of presenting the gospel to nonbelievers. Another case that illustrates this is the IDSAD project of Nicaragua presented by Uriel Tercero, where he is working at sustainable agriculture as a basis for holistic community development. In this case there is a clear relationship between biblical reflection and agricultural practices.

Summing Up

To achieve effective management of holistic projects our work must include certain key aspects:

- ❖ Human resources are a key element of every process and require servant leadership, inspired by Jesus' model.
- ❖ Active and responsible community participation is important in the facilitation role of our organizations.

127

- ❖ Sustainable administrative and implementation systems will assure the continuity of our ministry and the community processes.
- ❖ Impact objectives are important for objectively measuring our effectiveness.
- ❖ To maintain a relevant ministry, the institution must develop mechanisms that adjust to the constant changes of the environment.
- ❖ Strategic thinking is important to provide meaning and continuity in our activities.
- ❖ We must be convinced that transformation in this world is an act of God. We are only collaborators.

REFERENCES

Jones, Laurie Beth. *Jesus, CEO: Using Ancient Wisdom for Visionary Leadership*. Hyperion, 1995.

Morrisey, George L. *Strategic Thinking: Building Your Planning Foundation*. San Francisco: Jossey-Bass, 1996.

Porter, Michael E. "What Is Strategy?" in *Harvard Business Review*, Vol. 74, Nov.-Dec. 1996.

Quinteros Uribe, Víctor Manuel. *Evaluacion de Proyectos Sociales: Construccion de Indicadores*. Colombia: Fundación FES, 1996.

Weisbrod, Marin R. and Sandra Janoff. *Future Search: An Action Guide to Finding Common Ground in Organizations and Communities*. San Francisco: Berret-Koehler Publishers, 1995.

13
The holistic practitioner

Bryant L. Myers

Our cases tell us interesting and important things about how communities have entered into a journey of human transformation that involves material and spiritual change. One cannot read these stories without being struck by the importance of those Christian women and men who obeyed God's call to work among the poor. The role of the holistic practitioner[1] is important. It would be hard to believe these cases were possible without these people.

Our consultation in Quito decided to spend some time reflecting on the holistic practitioner. Based on the experience of those present, we asked what holistic practitioners need to know, what kind of character they need to have, what technical skills they need to possess and what attitudes of the heart will make them effective. The purpose of this brief chapter is to share those reflections.

I will begin by offering an alternative biblical framework for evangelism and Christian witness which I think is more helpful to the relief and development worker than the traditional evangelical framework of "Go and make disciples of all nations" (Matthew 28:19). While the Great Commission is true and right, it is not the only point of departure for mission and it does not fit the relief and development agency as well as it does a traditional mission agency.

I will then present our findings on the holistic practitioner using the following categories:

- ❖ They are Christians
- ❖ They have Christian character
- ❖ They are professional

This chapter will then close with some remarks on the formation and development of the holistic practitioner.

AN ALTERNATIVE BIBLICAL FRAMEWORK FOR CHRISTIAN WITNESS

A careful examination of the narrative of the book of Acts reveals an interesting pattern. Evangelism—the verbal declaration of the good news of Jesus Christ—often is the second act, not the first. Peter's powerful evangelistic sermon in Acts 2 begins with Peter saying, "Let me explain this to you." The "this" to which he refers is that the people of Jerusalem were hearing the disciples praise God "each . . . in his own language." The power of God in the coming of the Holy Spirit had caused the people to be "amazed and perplexed." Peter's unplanned sermon was an extemporaneous response to their question, "What does this mean?"

In Acts 3, Peter again makes an unplanned declaration of the gospel. The people on the temple mount were filled with "wonder and amazement" when they see the former crippled beggar walking about praising God. Peter begins his sermon by asking, "Men of Israel, why does this surprise you?"

In Acts 7, a man named Saul hears the gospel for the first time when he hears Stephen answer the question of the Sanhedrin, "Are these charges true?" Stephen reframes the history of Israel so that it culminates in the good news of Jesus, the Christ. The Sanhedrin was asking about charges resulting from the signs and wonders God did through Stephen (Acts 6:8).

In each case, the declaration of the gospel is preceded by evidence of the power and work of God in the lives of people. Deeds, unusual and unexpected, provoked questions among the people— questions to which the gospel was the answer.

One natural framework for thinking about evangelism done by a Christian relief and development agency or a local church doing holistic mission in its community is in a way that provokes questions to which the gospel is the answer. When water is found in the desert, when children no longer die from diarrhea, when unproductive land begins to produce food, when drinking and family violence give way to harmony and working together, surely this provokes a question: What is the cause of these miracles? The answer to this question points to the activity and character of the God of the Bible and his redemptive work in a fallen world. Those we help demand the Good News from us. In a sense, this is a developmental approach to evangelism.

This framework challenges the way evangelicals have traditionally thought about evangelism. When the framework was "go and tell" and people did not respond, we blamed the devil or the people themselves by saying, "They have hard hearts." The framework of provoking the question causes us to wonder if we are at fault when no one asks us questions to which the gospel is the answer. Thus, the burden is on us, not on those we wish to reach. Also, instead of limiting our Christian witness training to how to *say* the gospel, we now expand the scope of our training so that it creates and nurtures holistic disciples whose lives and actions are more likely to provoke the question we long to answer.

The relief and development effort now has a Christian witness framework. We seek to promote human transformation, community ownership and structural change in ways that we hope the Holy Spirit may use to provoke questions to which the gospel is the answer. We now understand that Christian witness is part of what we do, how we do it and how we act. We realize that we are always witnessing. The only question is, To what are we witnessing? Everything we do can be done in a kingdom-like way and, if done so, may be used to trigger the question we would most like to answer.

So the key to holistic ministry is not so much in the program activities as it is in the people who do them. We are the message, or at least we can cause people to raise the question. Holism is first and foremost in the development promoter or community organizer, not in the program. For this reason, we must pay special attention to the formation and characteristics of holistic practitioners.

131

WHO THEN ARE HOLISTIC PRACTITIONERS?

They are Christians

You cannot witness to something that you are not. Holistic practitioners must be committed Christians. This is obvious, but it is not enough. Holistic practitioners must also be holistic disciples. They must love God with all their heart, mind, soul and strength, and they must love their neighbors as they love themselves. They must understand that God's rule extends to all of life—our relationship with God, ourselves, our neighbors and our environment. They must be committed to being obedient to God's call to live out that rule. They must understand the bias of the gospel in favor of the lost, the poor, the forgotten, the ignored and the exploited. They must desire to share the best news that they have, the good news of Jesus Christ.

But being Christian means much more. Holistic practitioners must have a passion for developing a truly biblical worldview. This means becoming increasingly aware of the modern (or sometimes traditional) worldview to which their education and socialization makes them captive. This means understanding how this non-biblical worldview influences their understanding of poverty and their view of the better future they desire for themselves and the communities with which they work. This means working hard to recreate a truly biblical worldview that is holistic, includes the supernatural and has room for all the good of modern science.

They have Christian character

Holistic practitioners need a strong Christian character, one that thinks more highly of others than of themselves. They must have a love of the poor and a sense of call to serve those on society's margin. They must be able to see the image of God in even the most desperate and believe that God's image is the truth about this person. They must believe that God has given gifts to the poor that can be called out and used by the poor for their own transformation. The poor must be granted the same voice and dignity the holistic practitioner wishes for himself or herself. Holistic practitioners must believe that when all is said and done, poor people have as much potential and can be as effective as any other human being.

Holistic practitioners must be reliable and honest, demonstrating the fruit of the Spirit. They must believe in the transformative power of good relationships and seek to become friends with those they serve. They must be transparent, ever willing to speak of their strengths and weaknesses, always bearing witness to God as the source of their strengths and the means by which they overcome their weaknesses.

Holistic practitioners must have that genuine humility that being in Christ allows, the balanced humility that affirms the worth and gifts that God has given the holistic practitioner and also owns the weaknesses and sin that work to undermine their Christian life. They must understand themselves as stewards, stewards of the gifts God has given them, stewards of their relationships with the poor, stewards of the resources they bring to the community and that the community already has.

They must be professional

When God finished the work of the Creation, only one measure was employed to assess God's work: it was good. God likes good work and so must we. We should never believe or act as if being a Christian is an excuse to be amateurish in our work. There should be no dichotomy between being Christian and being professional.

Holistic practitioners must develop a deep understanding of the complexity of poverty and its many dimensions and expressions. They must use the lessons of the social sciences and of Scripture to understand the causes of poverty—material, spiritual, cultural and sociopolitical. They must develop sophisticated understandings of the local socio-political-economic-religious context and how this context works for and against the well-being of the poor and those on the margin.

All of this must be done with the profound understanding that the community understands its reality in ways that are often deeper and more accurate than that of any outsider. Balancing the need to learn from the community and to take its indigenous knowledge seriously with the equally valid fact that the holistic practitioner brings information and knowledge the community needs is a serious and continuing challenge. This is where a truly Christian character is so important. We come with gifts God gave us to add to the gifts God has already placed in the community; there is no room for superiority or pride.

Holistic practitioners need to develop skills for working with communities in a way that empowers and liberates. They need to learn the skills of community organizing. They need to learn how to learn what the community already knows. They need to understand the basics of community-based health care, sustainable agriculture, water management, microenterprise development. They need to understand and develop sustainable development systems linking families and communities with local governmental, business and religious institutions so that life-enhancing relationships are formed. They need to understand the principles and skills of popular education that enable learning to take place at the direction and pace of the community.

Holistic practitioners need to understand and appreciate the importance of worldview and its impact on development. They need to understand values and how values are formed and changed. They must understand how the community understands cause and effect and how to help the community move from its traditional or modern worldview toward a more biblical one. This is very difficult work, because the worldview of the holistic practitioner is often not biblical as well. Helping people move from their traditional worldview while one suffers from a modern scientific one is not an easy task. Both the practitioner and the community are seeking a worldview that has the God of the Bible at its center. This implies that each has something to learn from the other, and that both must change.

Holistic practitioners must acknowledge that they do not know all they need to know. They must be learners who are always seeking new insights from Scripture and from the community. They must be people who document, who ask questions, who listen to the stories of the people and then spend time with the people in reflection. What have we learned? What worked? What did not? What did we miss? What is God saying to us in all this?

THE IMPORTANCE OF FORMATION

Now we have to be realistic. Where do we find these paragons of virtue? Who can meet these standards? No one can. What we have described is a composite of the best that we can imagine based on what our experience and Scripture teach us. No individual will be what we have described.

This is why formation is so important. Selecting people with the right gifts and character and then intentionally and systematically providing for their training and formation is the key to developing the holistic practitioner who can promote or facilitate transformational development. Our description suggests that we need to think of formation as disciple-making, of developing mature Christians with the best professional skills possible.

The local church or the relief and development agency must define the attitudes, behaviors and skills that holistic practitioners need, and then provide holistic practitioners with opportunities to acquire these through formal training, hands-on experience and mentoring. There should be no dichotomy between spiritual formation and professional training; both are inseparable parts of developing the holistic practitioner. This means that spiritual formation, learning the spiritual disciplines, and becoming competent in popular education and community organizing are all part of the formation of the holistic practitioner.

Finally, we must release the holistic practitioner from the demand, either from us or from within themselves, to be successful. Following Jesus is about obedience, not success. Holistic practitioners who sacrifice everything—themselves, their marriages, the well-being of their children—to be successful among the poor are making idols of the poor, not serving God. We have a responsibility to free them to make a gift of themselves, their character and their skills in all their relationships, beginning with the ones at home.

NOTE

1 I first heard this name for the Christians who promote basic transformational development from Dr. Sam Kamaleson, former vice president for pastor's conferences and special ministries at World Vision International, now retired.

Part three

Conclusion

14
What have we learned?

Bryant L. Myers

What can we say at the end of the day about holistic relief and development in Latin America? What lessons can we draw from the nine cases studies and the insightful comments from the perspectives of theology, management and the formation of holistic practitioners?

Relief and development are difficult tasks, and each experience is deeply embedded in a particular context and, hence, shaped by it. Comparing a street children's ministry in modern Curitiba to one with farmers in the highlands of Bolivia to a Christian hospital outreach program in Honduras is a dangerous process indeed. Whatever I might say must be treated with care; it will not bear much weight.

I will begin by making comments on the understanding of holistic ministry reflected in the cases. In particular, I want to discuss the following topics:

- ❖ A holistic understanding of poverty
- ❖ A holistic view of a better future
- ❖ A holistic view of Christian witness
- ❖ Sustainable transformation

I will then close with a discussion of the role and importance of the local church, one of the most interesting features of some of these cases. In particular, I will comment on:

- ❖ The role of the church
- ❖ The role of the parachurch agency
- ❖ Evaluating the quality of the church

UNDERSTANDING OF HOLISTIC MINISTRY

These cases display a consistently holistic mindset in the way poverty is described and understood, as well as the implicit view of the better future toward which the community wishes to move.

A holistic understanding of poverty

A holistic understanding of poverty must be complex and nuanced. Poverty is material. Poverty is also social or structural. Poverty is spiritual. Furthermore, all the factors that lead to poverty are interconnected and influence each other.

Too often, the materialistic modern worldview traps us into defining poverty in material terms: people are poor because they do not have certain things—enough food, potable water, productive land, money and the like. This leads to a development approach that provides the things people are missing. Or a material understanding of poverty causes us to understand poverty as the absence of the right skills or knowledge—how to use improved seeds, managing rain run-off, purifying water, managing a microenterprise. This view tends to limit our development options to skills training, education and demonstration programs.

This view of poverty, while true, is not sufficient. It ignores the impact of social systems and culture. Sometimes poverty is linked to the fact that the social system denies access to the poor: they cannot use good land; they cannot afford school fees so their children do not go to school; they are denied access to markets, credit, extension information and the like. Sometimes culture works against development, as is the case when fiestas and parties are the social norm, or when girls are not allowed to go to school. The Latin American culture of *machismo* undermines the productive role of the male and marginalizes the female.

Finally, there are issues of the spirit, which can cause and reinforce poverty. Fear of local gods, shamans and the spirits work against innovation. The mindset that poverty is the will of God, something that must be accepted as one's lot in life, is anti-developmental. Immorality and misuse of drugs and alcohol sap strength, financial resources and the will to change.

These cases are remarkable in the fact that all these factors tend to be part of the description of what it is that needs transformation.

Material needs are regularly described. In all the cases, we observe malnutrition and the lack of food, poor land and low food production, lack of medicine and illness, lack of shelter and a place to sleep, and lack of clean water. Poverty is the absence of things.

The absence of knowledge is also given its due. In CORCRIDE (Honduras) and IDSAD (Nicaragua), we learn of the need to educate about deforestation and soil degradation. The Redeemer Project (Brazil) points to the need for technical skills among the homeless, as well as adequate schooling. All the projects have heavy training and education components.

Cultural barriers to development are mentioned frequently. The project in Juntavi, Bolivia points to the poverty-causing and reinforcing role of fiestas. The Redeemer Project announces the mitigating role of the concentration of wealth and land ownership. The Christian Social Project in Colombia describes the low view of women in the culture and the church. BEM (Brazil) mentions the controlling power of *caudalismo* (the willingness to follow a leader who has charisma). CORCRIDE and BEM report the failure of culture as families disintegrate under the pressure of poverty.

Spiritual needs are declared clearly. CORCRIDE and IDSAD mention alcoholism, drug use and immorality. BEM mentions family disintegration, incest, prostitution and idolatry (toward the saints). The project in Juntavi points to animism, fear of spirits, alcohol and violence. The cell groups case in Lima points to the role poverty plays in reducing life to meeting today's basic needs, eroding any aspirations for the future. All of the cases measure spiritual need in terms of people needing to know the saving and transforming power of Jesus Christ.

The causes of poverty in the cases are also described holistically. Sometimes the cause is located in nature—natural calamities or poor soil. Other times the cause is described as being within the

141

poor themselves—poor choices, immoral habits. At other times the cause is within the culture—fiestas, shamans, gods and spirits. And sometimes the cause lies within the social system—patterns of land ownership, access to resources and the like. In the two urban cases (the Office for Social Advancement and Development in Barranquilla and the cell groups ministry in Lima), the loss of their cultural heritage by those arriving in the city from the countryside is a primary cause of their poverty.

A holistic view of a better future

When we understand poverty holistically, we tend to envision the community's better future in a holistic way as well. The goals and outcomes of the program go beyond meeting physical need, and even providing education. Cultural, social and spiritual change become part of the vision.

The implicit view of the better future in these cases can also be described as a better future for individuals, families and the community, as well as encompassing the social, cultural and spiritual realms. And so they should. After all, the kingdom of God is ultimately about enhancing life—affirming those things that enhance life and working against those things that devalue or limit life. The whole gospel is about living with God and living the fruitful life of a faithful steward with your family and as part of your community.

At the personal level, the cases speak frequently about the importance of new personal habits and ethical behavior. Working together, sharing, less drinking and violence are mentioned frequently. The cell group discipling process in Lima works specifically on this, but most cases allude to this positive impact of the gospel. The cases generally show a real concern for the kinds of Christians that are resulting from these ministries. The goal is that Christians will engage in the whole of community life, including leadership and caregiving.

Cultural change is also frequently alluded to. IDSAD in Nicaragua speaks of seeking an impact on social life, with bars closing and fights ceasing, and of an emerging local philanthropy that is feeding children and opening schools. The project in Juntavi seeks a community organization that works for the community's well-being. BEM in Brazil speaks of the desire for responsible families, growing their own food and taking care of their own families. The Christian Social Project in Bolivia seeks to develop women who will play a full role in all aspects of community life—social, political, economic and religious.

Spiritual transformation is also a major focus. Working against anti-life festivals and trying to formulate Christian alternatives is an important factor in Juntavi. Attending worship, studying the Bible and the importance of prayer are all part of what the better human future requires. A better future means being freed from the fear of spirits and the fatalism of animistic belief.

In many of the cases, it is gratifying to see that the view of the better future includes a growing church fully engaged in and part of the life of the community. These cases take the church's role in the transformational process and its importance as part of the community's better future as a given. This is something that distinguishes these cases from our earlier collections from Asia and Africa.[1] But more on this later.

A holistic view of Christian witness

In Mark's gospel, the twelve disciples were called first and foremost to "be with Jesus." Any good news we have for others begins and finds its life in our relationship with Jesus. These twelve were called to be with Jesus, we are told, so that they could preach and cast out demons (Mark 3:14-15). When the disciples returned from their first solo ministry journey, they reported preaching the Good News, casting out demons and healing the sick (Mark 6). The gospel is life, deed, word and sign. All are aspects of the one gospel message. And so it is in our cases.

There is a recurring focus on the life of Christians together, together in worship and in ministry. Often we see the importance of prayer, discipleship, studying the Bible together and, in the case of the Redeemer Project, an emphasis on spirituality derived from the traditions of the Church Fathers. Being with Jesus and with his body is the beginning of transformational ministry. Over and over,

143

the cases start with the conversion of the church or some of its members. The poor were always there, but now the church has the eyes to see them and the ears to hear their cry. This was the case in the Redeemer Project in Brazil, the Assemblies of God (IDSAD) in Nicaragua, Juntavi in Bolivia, CORCRIDE in Honduras and the Evangelical Hospital in Honduras.

Saying the words of the gospel are part of every case. People are always talking about Jesus and what Jesus has done and can do. In the stories of Christians or churches working with the communities to address their physical, cultural and social needs, their evangelistic intent is clear. Yet, these words were almost always expressed in the context of personal relationships of trust and appreciation. Friend-ships, walking together, seeking out the forgotten and invisible and learning their names, praying and Bible study by small groups fre-quently found expression in our cases. There is an unmistakable emphasis on the power of transformative relationships as the con-text in which the words of the gospel are expressed and heard.

Yet, deeds were the most frequent illustration of the transforma-tive nature of the gospel, as one would expect from cases describ-ing Christian relief and development. The author of the cell group case study put it this way: "Expressing love in a practical manner, evangelizing through lifestyle and acts of compassion that others can see." Formerly treeless, poorly producing land returns to sus-tainable life in Nicaragua. A poor, hungry community becomes self-sufficient in food in Bolivia. Alternative communities are cre-ated in which urban dwellers can find a place and a sense of belonging in the city slums, as in the cell group case from Lima. Clean water, more food, less illness, recovered homeless and street children off drugs and in school.

As important, however, in considering witness as deed is the role of the Christian in the development process itself. Quality profes-sional work by Christians is a powerful positive witness. A profes-sional, high quality health service, modestly carried out, was the key to the Evangelical Hospital in Honduras. The best witness occurs when a quality spiritual life is accompanied by quality pro-fessional skills. God likes quality work and so do the poor.

Signs and wonders surface as part of the work of the gospel in these cases. Healing and delivery from alcohol and drugs were mentioned in IDSAD in Nicaragua. Fiestas were transformed into Christian gatherings for thanksgiving in Juntavi. Marriages have recovered in Lima as drinking was overcome and family violence subsided. "We understand our great need for the power and anointing of the Holy Spirit to confront and triumph over the powers of this world, both visible and invisible," comes the call from the Redeemer Project in Brazil.

The bottom line seems simple: When Christians live with the people, witnessing by life, deed, word and sign, the poor are transformed and churches grow.

Sustainable transformation

One of the important new dimensions of our thinking about transformational development is the issue of sustainability. What kinds of things contribute to making change sustainable? What enables a work to carry on in the future without the help of the outside agency? We get some hints in our cases.

Leadership is a factor, as we might expect. Without developing local leadership, sustainability is hard to imagine. One of the chapters in this book quotes John Perkins: "Developing creative leaders is both the most essential and the most difficult part of Christian community development."[2] The importance of leadership in Juntavi is obvious; the three Christian men encourage people to work hard, act responsibly, save money and avoid fiestas. In IDSAD, the Christian leaders are the source of helping people make better use of land and sustainable agriculture. In the cases of the Redeemer Project, the Lima cell groups and IDSAD, local Christian leaders encourage local philanthropy and tithing as a means of economic sustainability for ongoing programs.

Microenterprise also seems an inescapable factor for sustainability. Some cases center their whole transformational program on microenterprise, such as the Office for Social Advancement and Development in Barranquilla and the Christian Social Project case from Cali, Colombia.

In many of the cases, the presence of a spiritually alive, socially active church or Christian agency, like the Evangelical Hospital in Honduras, seems integral to sustaining the energy, human resources and funding for the program. More on the local church later.

Interestingly, money is not mentioned as a factor in sustainability. In the case of CORCRIDE, the case writer makes the specific claim that their experience of uncertain funding simply strengthened the program. The key to sustainability is committed people, not money.

THE CRITICAL ROLE OF THE CHURCH

The conversation on sustainability cannot be complete without reflecting on the role of the church in these cases. In most cases, the church is both the agent of change and the hope for the future. After reading these cases, one can hardly escape the conclusion that a spiritually alive, socially engaged church is a key to causing and sustaining true transformation. More than in our two earlier consultations, this consultation featured cases in which the active partner was a church, or an agency of local churches, in contrast to an outside parachurch agency.

One of the cases quotes the bold claim of Indian relief and development thinker Vishal Mongalwadi: "If God were to create a PVO [NGO], it would be the church." Why should this be? A church that truly lives out the whole of the gospel message will hear the voices of those whose lives are not what God intends them to be. Such a church will understand poverty holistically and will respond in kind. Many of our cases are the stories of Christians and churches who have made this discovery.

C. René Padilla, in his theological reflection, calls our attention to the fact that holistic mission means the church's full participation in the social and political life of the community. This is what is meant by being salt and light, he claims. In our cases, church leaders become community leaders (for example, a mayor in a Bolivian village). The Evangelical Hospital in Honduras has an accepted role in its city, providing jobs, health services by extension, local training and the like. In the BEM project in Brazil and IDSAD in Nicaragua, we see Christians deliberately involving themselves in community affairs.

Churches in the case of CORCRIDE in Honduras emphasized the key role of lay people using their professional skills for the good of the community. The Assemblies of God churches in Nicaragua mobilized local volunteers from among the churches. Over and over, we heard that the caring work of the church in the life of the community overcame the fear and suspicion many hold for the church in Latin America.

Not all churches are up to this high calling. When churches do not understand this holistic call of the gospel, they often become part of the problem. The chapter on the IDSAD case says, "In the past the community thought that the only thing the church did was have worship services." The church members of the Redeemer Project in Brazil spoke of the need for their conversion from self-centeredness to being concerned for the poor.

The consultation participants spoke honestly of the complicity of the Latin American church in the poverty and exploitation of the region, and did not limit criticism to the Roman Catholic Church. There was frank talk of the blindness of Protestant churches, who too often teach and practice a vertical gospel rich in its focus on God but without regard for the community just outside its doors. Participants spoke prophetically of the risk the Pentecostal and charismatic churches face of practicing a gospel so heavenly-oriented that it is of no earthly use, and praised God for the example of the Assemblies of God churches in northern Nicaragua.

This critical role of the local church(es) in transformational development raises the issue of the role and responsibility of parachurch groups. In the cases of CORCRIDE, the Evangelical Hospital and IDSAD, parachurch groups saw themselves as servants of the local churches, and were very intentional in their desire to strengthen the social outreach of the local churches. The Office for Social Advancement and Development viewed the involvement of the seven local churches as instrumental to their program's success. This relationship between the parachurch agency and the local church is an important partnership. Padilla reminds us that "parachurch organizations find their reason for existence to the extent that they foster the church's organic growth and empower local churches for holistic mission."

One final word on the local church and its role in the community's transformation. Evaluating the success of holistic ministry where the local church is involved is a little different from evaluating a relief and development agency. Since the relief and development agency is not a permanent part of the community, it can limit its evaluation to program effectiveness—goals achieved, evidence of community ownership, indicators of value change and the like. A local church needs to assess these things, but must also assess the impact of the transformational process on itself. Is the local church growing in a kingdom-like way or not?

This is where Padilla offers an important suggestion on an evaluative framework for the local church doing holistic mission. He reminds us of the holistic assessment of church growth that Orlando E. Costas proposed in the early 1980s. Costas suggested that local churches involved in holistic mission need to look at four dimensions of growth:

1. Numerical growth measured by conversions, baptisms, or new members.
2. Organic growth measured by the quality of relationships among church members, financial health of the congregation, quality of worship and celebration.
3. Conceptual growth measured by understanding of the meaning and implications of the gospel, knowledge and application of Scripture, and understanding of the context in which the church and its members live.
4. Diaconal growth measured by the incarnational ministry of the church in the world, serving the poor and those in need as a sign of God's redemptive love.

I believe this evaluative framework holds promise. If a vital local church is a necessary element for the sustainability of any transformational development program, then the relief and development agency must join in true partnership with local churches and be dissatisfied with the results of its work until two sets of standards are met: the agency's own professional standards, and a local church that meets the terms of Costas' framework for holistic church growth.

A FINAL WORD

That local churches are passionately and sacrificially involved in the whole of the life of their communities is the best news of this consultation. It is not just parachurch groups or individual Christians caring for the poor, but local congregations serving God by working for the betterment of their own communities. Even better, some of the cases involved Pentecostal and charismatic churches. If this fast-growing and increasingly influential part of the Latin American church can emulate the kind of holistic ministry illustrated in these cases, then a major force for social and spiritual change will be released across the continent.

NOTES

1 Tetsunao Yamamori, Bryant L. Myers and David Conner, eds., *Serving with the Poor in Asia* (Monrovia: MARC Publications, 1995), and Tetsunao Yamamori, Bryant L. Myers, Kwame Bediako and Larry Reed, eds., *Serving with the Poor in Africa* (Monrovia: MARC Publications, 1996).

2 John M. Perkins, *Beyond Charity: The Call to Christian Community Development* (Grand Rapids: Baker Book House, 1993), p. 74.

Part four

Appendixes

Appendix A:
Consultation participants

Some 24 practitioners, theorists and representatives gathered in Quito, Ecuador, in November 1996 to discuss effective holistic ministry in Latin America. Following is a list of participants, their affiliations and the countries in which they are based.

Name	Organization	Country
Alexis Andino	Regional Christian Comm. for Development	Honduras
Débra de Arco	World Vision	Colombia
David Bussau	Opportunity Foundation Limited	Australia
Rosa Camargo	Office for Social Advancement & Development	Colombia
Luis Cesair	Pastor in Montevideo	Uruguay
Alva Couto	POLUS Institute	Brazil
Ivan Delgado	Food for the Hungry International	Bolivia
Kenneth Ekström	Food for the Hungry International	Nicaragua
David Evans	Food for the Hungry International	U.S.A.
Milly Lugo	Fieldstead Institute	U.S.A.
Denise da Silva Maranháo	Bem Estar do Menor	Brazil
Enrique Martínez	Evangelical Hospital Siguatepeque	Honduras
Javier Mayorga	World Vision	Costa Rica
Bryant L. Myers	World Vision	U.S.A.
Claudio F. Oliver	The Redeemer Project	Brazil
Jim Oehrig	MAP Latin America	Ecuador
C. René Padilla	KAIROS	Argentina
Atilio Quintanilla	Food for the Hungry International	Peru

Name	Organization	Country
Gregory Rake	Mennonite Board of Missions	U.S.A.
Diana Schmierer	Fieldstead Institute	U.S.A.
Don Schmierer	Fieldstead Institute	U.S.A.
Mauricio Solís	MAP Latin America	Ecuador
Uriel Tercero	Social Development Institute/Assemblies of God	Nicaragua
Tetsunao Yamamori	Food for the Hungry International	U.S.A.

Appendix B:
Case study guidelines

Holistic ministry practitioners attending the November 1996 consultation in Quito, Ecuador, wrote case studies of effective holistic ministry in Latin America. The authors used the following guidelines.

1. Acquaint yourself with the concept of holistic ministry.

Although reconciliation with others is not reconciliation with God, nor is social action evangelism, nor is political liberation salvation, nevertheless we affirm that evangelism and sociopolitical involvement are both part of our Christian duty.

Both are necessary expressions of our doctrines of God and humanity, our love for our neighbor and our obedience to Jesus Christ (see section five of the Lausanne Covenant). Tetsunao Yamamori expresses this concept as follows:

> Ministering to physical needs and ministering to spiritual needs, though functionally separate, are relationally inseparable, and both are essential to the total ministry of Christ's church.

2. Provide the context of your case study.

Describe the people group with whom you have done your work. What is their history as a people group? In what material and spiritual ways were they poor? What are the causes of their material poverty? Spiritual poverty? Social poverty?

3. Describe your holistic ministry program.

What type of development project did you implement (water, food production, health, microenterprise, integrated development)? Describe it in some detail. How did it come into being? What kind of development process did you use? How was or were the church(es) involved? How was Christian witness to take place?

4. What were the results?

What kind of material or physical transformation has taken place? How have the lives of the poor improved? What evidence of spiritual transformation in people and in the community have you seen? What evidence of cultural or social transformation have you seen?

5. Describe the results of people deepening their relationship with or coming to know Christ.

What has happened in spiritual terms among the people? What evidence can you cite that demonstrates that evangelism or renewal is taking place? How was the local church involved? Is the spiritual change limited to individuals? A particular church? The community as a whole? Are churches growing? How are Christians becoming part of the social transformation of their communities?

6. Identify the factors that contributed to the emergence or growth of a Christ group (a growing church or a new group of believers).

How did the development project contribute to evangelism or renewal in the community? What role did the development agency staff play, if any? What training did the development agency staff have in terms of Christian witness?

7. Evaluate your case study.

Looking back on your history with this project, are there things you would have done differently? What obstacles prevented full success? What hindered the results of the spiritual ministry?

**MARC**

Bringing you key resources on the world mission of the church

MARC books and other publications support the work of MARC (Mission Advanced Research and Communications Center), which is to inspire vision and empower Christian mission among those who extend the whole gospel to the whole world.

Also in the Cases in Holistic Ministry series:

▶ *Serving With the Poor in Africa: Cases in Holistic Ministry,* T. Yamamori, B. Myers, K. Bediako & L. Reed, editors. Real holistic ministry cases are presented from throughout Africa. Commentary and analysis on such topics as holistic healing, AIDS and evangelism deepens your understanding of holism. $15.95

▶ *Serving With the Poor in Asia,* T. Yamamori, B. Myers & D. Conner, editors. Cases are presented from seven different Asian contexts. Analysis and commentary reveal how holism impacts anthropology, theology and other disciplines. $15.95

▶ *By Word, Work and Wonder,* by Thomas H. McAlpine. Case studies from around the world focus on innovative mission practices and expand the range of issues surrounding the role of holism. $15.95

Other new MARC resources:

▶ *The New Context of World Mission* by Bryant L. Myers. A thorough yet concise visual portrayal of the entire sweep of Christian mission. Full-color graphics and up-to-date statistics show you where mission has been and where it's heading.

    Book... $ 8.95
    Slides.. $149.95
    Overheads....................................... $149.95
    Presentation Set *(one book, slides and overheads)* $249.00

▶ *With an Eye on the Future: Development and Mission in the 21st Century,* Duane Elmer & Lois McKinney, editors. Cutting-edge thinkers present essays in the fields of mission, development and church leadership that propose new strategies in the areas that will be vital to mission in the next century. $24.95

▶ *Street Children: A Guide to Effective Ministry*, Phyllis Kilbourn, editor. Uniquely designed to orient workers among street children. Several examples are given from every continent that show who street children are, why they are on the streets and what can be done in response to this global crisis. $23.95

▶ *Healing the Children of War*. A practical handbook for ministry to children who have suffered deep traumas. Examines the impact of war on children; the grieving child; forgiveness; restoring hope to the child; and many other important issues that surround children who have been victimized by war. $21.95

▶ *Children in Crisis: A New Commitment*. Alerts you to the multiple ways in which children are suffering around the world—AIDS, abandonment, abuse, forced labor, girl child—and equips you to respond in biblical ways. $21.95

Coming soon:

▶ *Mission Handbook 1998-2000*, John A. Siewert & Edna G. Valdez, editors. The most comprehensive guide to mission organizations in North America. Updated listings tell you everything you need to know about mission agencies in the U.S. and Canada: countries of service, types of ministry, financial data, contact information including phone and fax numbers, e-mail addresses and web site URLs. The latest mission trends and analysis provide important information for strategic mission planners. $49.95

Contact us toll free in the USA: 1-800-777-7752
Direct: (626) 301-7720

MARC A division of World Vision
800 W. Chestnut Ave. • Monrovia • CA • 91016-3198 • USA

Ask for the MARC Newsletter and complete publications list